Cycling in the YORKSHIRE DALES

TED SMART

This edition produced for The Book People Ltd
Hall Wood Avenue, Haydock,
St Helens WA11 9UL

Published by Collins
An imprint of HarperCollins*Publishers*
77-85 Fulham Palace Road
London W6 8JB

First published 1999

Routes compiled by Neil Wheadon.
Design by Creative Matters Design Consultancy, Glasgow.
Typeset by Bob Vickers.

Photographs reproduced by kind permission of the following:
Image Bank pages 18 (Simon Wilkinson), 24 (Carlos Navajas), 59 (Antony Edwards), 67 (Carlos Navajas), 87 (Simon Wilkinson); John Morrison pages 5, 11, 32, 35, 43, 47, 48, 55, 62, 71, 79, 82, 90, 95, 97, 111; Neil Wheadon page 51; Andy Williams pages 8, 30, 39, 40, 44, 101.

The landscape is changing all the time. While every care has been taken in the preparation of this guide, the Publisher accepts no responsibility whatsoever for any loss, damage, injury or inconvenience sustained or caused as a result of using this guide.

Printed in Scotland

ISBN 0583 34014 8
99/1/15

CONTENTS

KEY TO ROUTES

Distances have been rounded up or down to the nearest 0.5km (mile).

Route colour coding

undemanding rides compiled specifically with families in mind
15–25km (10–15 miles)

middle distance rides suitable for all cyclists
25–40km (15–25 miles)

half-day rides for the more experienced and adventurous cyclist
40–60km (25–40 miles)

challenging full-day rides
over 60km (over 40 miles)

grande randonnée – a grand cycling tour
100km (60 miles)

Routes marked with this symbol are off-road or have off-road sections
(includes well-surfaced cycleways as well as rougher off-road tracks)

Yorkshire Dales National Park

LOCATION MAP

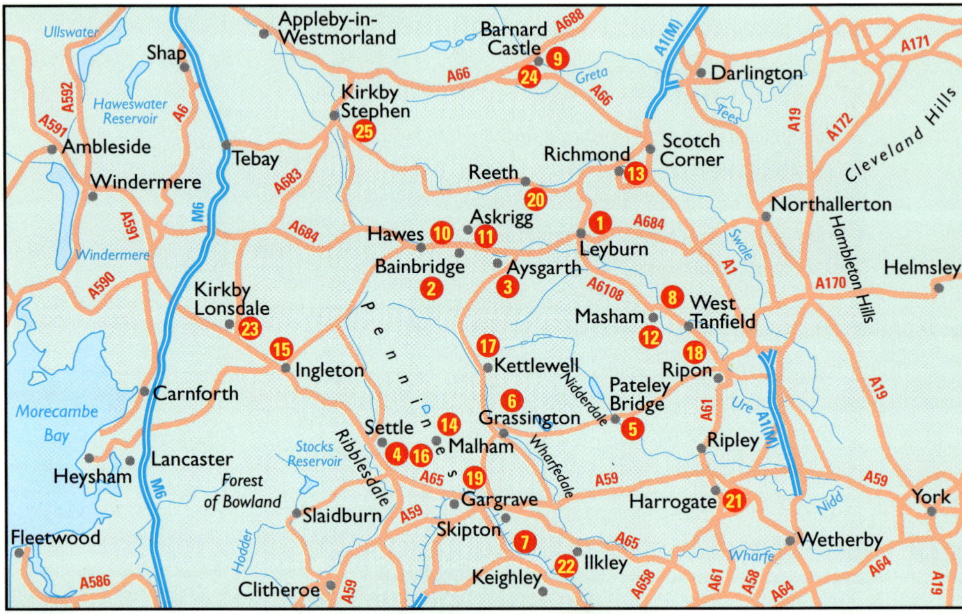

KEY TO ROUTE MAPS

M23	Motorway
A259	'A' road / Dual carriageway
B2130	'B' road / Dual carriageway
	Good minor road
	Minor road
	Track / bridleway
	Railway / station
	Canal / river
	Lake
50	Contour (height in metres)
	Cycle route / Optional route
	Start of cycle route
12	Route direction
B	Place of interest
	Public house
	Café / refreshments
	Restaurant
	Convenience store
i	Tourist Information Centre
P	Parking
	Telephone
	Picnic site
	Camping site
	Public toilets
	Place of worship
	Viewpoint
	Golf course
	Tumulus
	Urban area
	Woodland

Height above sea level

metres	50	100	150	200	300	400	500	600	700	800	900 metres
feet	165	330	490	655	985	1315	1645	1975	2305	2635	2965 feet

INTRODUCTION

How to use this guide

Collins' *Cycling in the Yorkshire Dales* has been devised for those who want trips out on their bicycles along quiet roads and tracks, passing interesting places and convenient refreshment stops without having to devise their own routes. Each of the 25 routes in this book has been compiled and ridden by an experienced cyclist for cyclists of all abilities.

Cycling in the Yorkshire Dales is easy to use. Routes range from undemanding rides compiled specifically with families in mind to challenging full-day rides; the type of route is easily identified by colour coding (see page 5). At the start of each route an information box summarises: total distance (in kilometres/miles – distances have been rounded up or down throughout to the nearest 0.5km/mile and are approximate only); grade (easy, moderate or strenuous based on distance and difficulty); terrain; an average time to allow for the route; directions to the start of the route by car and, if appropriate, by train.

Each route is fully mapped and has concise, easy-to-follow directions. Comprehensive information on places of interest and convenient refreshment stops along each route are also given. Accumulated mileages within each route description give an indication of progress, while the profile diagram is a graphic representation of gradients along the route. These should be used as a guide only.

The following abbreviations are used in the route directions:

LHF	left hand fork
RHF	right hand fork
SO	straight on
SP	signpost
TJ	T junction
TL	turn left
TR	turn right
XR	crossroads

Cycling in the Yorkshire Dales

The rides in this book explore the Yorkshire Dales, and although not all of the routes stay within the confines of the Yorkshire Dales National Park, they cover an area from Barnard Castle in the north, to Skipton in the south, and from Ripon in the west as far as the M6 motorway to the east.

The routes are designed to stay away from busy main roads as much as possible and to allow cyclists to discover the peaceful back lanes, tracks, bridleways and cycleways that cross this area, passing all manner of museums, castles, historic houses and other attractions. Although the major roads are busy, particularly in summer, the minor roads have remarkably little traffic. The areas covered by these routes are still predominantly rural – many of the towns and villages have preserved their traditional character which you will see along the way.

Much of this area is hilly, and there are steep sections to be tackled in some of the routes. However, the effect is compensated for by the spectacular views – and you can always get off and push your bike!

Geology, geography and history

The Central Pennines are cut by a series of valleys – the area we know as the Yorkshire Dales. Five rivers, the Swale, Ure, Nidd, Wharfe and Aire, flow east from the northern and eastern Dales towards the North Sea. Another three rivers, the Ribble, Lune and Eden, start in the central moors and flow west towards the Irish Sea. In many cases, the rivers flow through limestone and the action of the moving water has carved deep clefts through the soft limestone to the harder, watertight slates and shales.

Approximately 300 million years ago, the land here was covered by the mud floor of a shallow tropical sea. The mud evolved into slate, the bedrock of many Dales rivers, and the remains of marine animals calcified, forming the limestone which gives the Dales its distinctive character. Gritstone, the hard rocks of the highest peaks, and the lower-level shale, were formed from the deposits of a huge river delta. As the land masses gradually moved, faults occurred and subterranean activity forced molten mineral solutions into the faults and cracks of the upper rocks – mostly lead but also some silver and gold. As the Ice Age retreated around 10,000 years BC, dams and lakes were formed and mud, made from the ground down rocks of the high tops, began to form the rich pastures of the central Dales. Today, the Yorkshire Dales are well-known for the classic limestone scenery – green pasture, limestone scars, screens and the natural limestone pavements – as well as the distinctive farmed landscape of flower-rich hay meadows, dry-stone walls and scattered barns, stone-built villages and wide expanses of moorland.

Typical Dales village

The Yorkshire Dales have been inhabited for thousands of years. Prehistoric hunters followed regular routes through the area. The Romans built roads, some of which are still used today, and began mining for lead. Drovers and pack-horsemen, moving animals and goods across the country, created green roads which can be traced for miles across the wild central moors. Corpse roads linked outlying hamlets to sanctified ground further down the Dale.

Farming and mining, expanded by the wealthy monasteries of the Middle Ages, were long the mainstay of the Dales economy. Today, farming and the more recent tourist industry play a vital role in the fortunes of the Dales.

The Yorkshire Dales National Park was formed in 1953 to protect the landscape from unsuitable development, allow public access and meet the needs of those who live and work in the area. It covers an area of approximately 1769 square km (683 square miles). The National Park Authority exercises planning control, provides information and park rangers, and maintains footpaths and bridleways. There are seven National Park Centres within the Park (see page 13); each provide information on all aspects of the park to visitors. Selected village post offices and shops also provide local information.

Preparing for a cycling trip

Basic maintenance

A cycle ride is an immense pleasure, particularly on a warm sunny day. Nothing is better than coasting along a country lane gazing over the countryside. Unfortunately, not every cycling day is as perfect as this, and it is important to make sure that your bike is in good order and that you are taking the necessary clothing and supplies with you.

Before you go out on your bicycle check that everything is in order. Pump the tyres up if needed, and check that the brakes are working properly and that nothing is loose – the brakes are the only means of stopping quickly and safely. If there is a problem and you are not sure that you can fix it, take the bike to a cycle repair shop – they can often deal with small repairs very quickly.

When you go out cycling it is important to take either a puncture repair kit or a spare inner tube – it is often quicker to replace the inner tube in the event of a puncture, though it may be a good idea to practise first. You also need a pump, and with a slow puncture the pump may be enough to get you home. To remove the tyre you need a set of tyre levers. Other basic tools are an Allen key and a spanner. Some wheels on modern bikes can be removed by quick release levers built into the bike. Take a lock for your bike and if you have to leave it at any time, leave it in public view and locked through the frame and front wheel to something secure.

What to wear and take with you

It is not necessary to buy specialised cycling clothes. If it is not warm enough to wear shorts wear trousers which are easy to move in but fairly close to the leg below the knee – leggings are ideal – as this stops the trousers catching the chain. If you haven't got narrow-legged trousers, bicycle clips will hold them in. Jeans are not a good idea as they are rather tight and difficult to cycle in, and if they get wet they take a long time to dry. If your shorts or trousers are thin you might get a bit sore from being too long on the saddle. This problem can be reduced by using a gel saddle, and by wearing thicker, or extra, pants. Once you are a committed cyclist you can buy cycling shorts; or undershorts which have a protective pad built in and which can be worn under anything. It is a good idea to wear several thin layers of clothes so that you can add or remove layers as necessary. A zip-fronted top gives easy temperature control. Make sure you have something warm and something waterproof.

If you wear shoes with a firm, flat sole you will be able to exert pressure on the pedals easily, and will have less work to do to make the bicycle move. Gloves not only keep your hands warm but protect them in the event that you come off, and cycling mittens which cushion your hands are not expensive. A helmet is not a legal requirement, but it will protect your head if you fall.

In general it is a good idea to wear bright clothing so that you can be easily seen by motorists, and this is particularly important when it is overcast or getting dark. If you might be out in the dark or twilight fit your bicycle with lights – by law your bicycle must have a reflector. You can also buy reflective bands for your ankles, or to wear over your shoulder and back, and these help motorists to see you.

You may be surprised how quickly you use up energy when cycling, and it is important to eat a carbohydrate meal before you set out. When planning a long ride, eat well the night before. You should eat small amounts of food regularly while you are cycling, or you may find that your energy suddenly disappears, particularly if there are hills or if the weather is cold. It is important to always carry something to eat with you – chocolate, bananas, biscuits – so that if you do start fading away you can restore yourself quickly. In warm weather you will sweat and use up fluid, and you always need to carry something to drink – water will do! Many bicycles have a fitment in which to put a water bottle, and if you don't have one a cycle shop should be able to fit one.

It is also a good idea to carry a small first aid kit. This should include elastoplasts or bandages, sunburn cream, and an anti-histamine in case you are stung by a passing insect.

It is a good idea to have a pannier to carry all these items. Some fit on the handlebars, some to the back of the seat and some onto a back rack. For a day's ride you probably won't need a lot of carrying capacity, but it is better to carry items in a pannier rather than in a rucksack on your back. Pack items that you are carrying carefully – loose items can be dangerous.

Getting to the start of the ride

If you are lucky you will be able to cycle to the start of the ride, but often transport is necessary. If you travel there by train, some sprinter services carry two bicycles without prior booking. Other services carry bicycles free in off-peak periods, but check the details with your local station. Alternatively, you could use your car – it may be possible to get a bike in the back of a hatchback if you take out the front wheel. There are inexpensive, easily fitted car racks which carry bicycles safely. Your local cycle store will be able to supply one to suit you.

Cycling on-road

Cycling on back roads is a delight with quiet lanes, interesting villages, good views and a smooth easy surface to coast along on. The cycle rides in this book are mainly on quiet roads but you sometimes cross busy roads or have stretches on B roads, and whatever sort of road you are on it is essential to ride safely. Always be aware of the possibility or existence of other traffic. Glance behind regularly, signal before you turn or change lane, and keep to the left. If there are motorists around, make sure that they have seen you before you cross their path. Cycling can be dangerous if you are competing for space with motor vehicles, many of which seem to have difficulty in seeing cyclists. When drivers are coming out of side

Swaledale

roads, catch their eye before you ride in front of them.

You will find that many roads have potholes and uneven edges. They are much more difficult to spot when you are in a group because of the restricted view ahead, and therefore warnings need to be given. It is a good idea to cycle about a metre out into the road, conditions permitting, so that you avoid the worst of the uneven surfaces and to give you room to move in to the left if you are closely overtaken by a motor vehicle.

Other things to be careful of are slippery roads, particularly where there is mud or fallen leaves. Sudden rain after a period of dry weather often makes the roads extremely slippery. Dogs, too, are a hazard because they often move unpredictably, and sometimes like to chase cyclists. If you are not happy, stop or go slowly until the problem has passed.

Pedalling

Many modern bikes have 18 or 21 gears with three rings at the front and six or seven on the back wheel, and for much of the time you will find that the middle gear at the front with the range of gears at the back will be fine. Use your gears to find one that is easy to pedal along in so that your feet move round easily and you do not put too much pressure on your knees. If you are new to the bike and the gears it is a good idea to practise changing the gears on a stretch of flat, quiet road so that when you need to change gears quickly you will be ready to do so.

Cycling in a group

When cycling in a group it is essential to do so in a disciplined manner for your own, and others', safety. Do not ride too close to the bicycle in front of you – keep about a bicycle's length between you so that you will have space to brake or stop. Always keep both hands on the handlebars, except when signalling, etc. It is alright to cycle two abreast on quiet roads, but if it is necessary to change from cycling two abreast to single file this is usually done by the outside rider falling in behind the nearside rider; always cycle in single file where there are double white lines, on busy roads, or on narrow and winding roads where you have a restricted view of the road ahead. Overtake on the right (outside) only; do not overtake on the inside.

It is important to pass information to other members of the group, for example:

car up – a vehicle is coming up behind the group and will be overtaking;

car down – a vehicle is coming towards the group;

single up – get into single file;

stopping – stopping, or

slowing/easy – slowing due to junction, etc., ahead;

on the left – there is an obstacle on the left, e.g. pedestrian, parked car;

pothole – pothole (and point towards it).

Accidents

In case of an accident, stay calm and, if needed, ring the emergency services on 999. It is a good idea to carry a basic first aid kit and perhaps also one of the commercial foil wraps to put around anyone who has an accident to keep them warm. If someone comes off their bicycle move them and the bike off the road if it is safe to do so. Get someone in the party to warn approaching traffic to slow down, and if necessary ring for an ambulance.

Cycling off-road

All the routes in this book take you along legal rights of way – bridleways, byways open to all traffic and roads used as public paths – it is illegal to cycle along footpaths. Generally the off-road sections of the routes will be easy if the weather and ground are dry. If the weather has been wet and the ground is muddy, it is not a good idea to cycle along bridleways unless you do not mind getting dirty and unless you have a mountain bike which will not get blocked up with mud. In dry weather any bicycle will be able to cover the bridleway sections, but you may need to dismount if the path is very uneven.

Off-road cycling is different to cycling on the road. The average speed is lower, you will use more energy, your riding style will be different and there is a different set of rules to obey – the off-road code:

1 Give way to horse riders and pedestrians, and use a bell or call out to warn someone of your presence.
2 Take your rubbish with you.
3 Do not light fires.
4 Close gates behind you.
5 Do not interfere with wildlife, plants or trees.
6 Use only tracks where you have a right of way, or where the landowner has given you permission to ride.
7 Avoid back wheel skids, which can start erosion gulleys and ruin the bridleway.

Some of the off-road rides take you some miles from shelter and civilisation – take waterproofs, plenty of food and drink and basic tools – especially spare inner tubes and tyre repair equipment. Tell someone where you are going and approximately when you are due back. You are more likely to tumble off your bike riding off-road, so you should consider wearing a helmet and mittens with padded palms.

Local Tourist Information Centres

Harrogate
Royal Baths Assembly Rooms, Harrogate
Telephone (01423) 537300

Horton-in-Ribblesdale
Penyghent Café, Horton-in-Ribblesdale
Telephone (01729) 860333

Ingleton
Community Centre, Ingleton
Telephone (015242) 41049

Kirkby Lonsdale
24 Main Street, Kirkby Lonsdale
Telephone (015242) 71437

Kirkby Stephen
Market Square, Kirkby Stephen
Telephone (017683) 71199

Pateley Bridge
14 High Street, Pateley Bridge
Telephone (01423) 711147

Richmond
Friary Gardens, Victoria Road, Richmond
Telephone (01748) 850252

Settle
Town Hall, Cheapside, Settle
Telephone (01729) 825192

Skipton
9 Sheep Street, Skipton
Telephone (01756) 792809

National Park Information Centres

Aysgarth Falls
Aysgarth Falls, Leyburn
Telephone (01969) 663424

Clapham
Clapham, Lancaster
Telephone (015242) 51419

Grassington
Hebden Road, Grassington
Telephone (01756) 752774

Hawes
Dales Countryside Museum, Station Road, Hawes
Telephone (01969) 667450

Malham
Malham, Skipton
Telephone (01729) 830363

Reeth
The Green, Reeth
Telephone (01748) 884059

Sedbergh
72 Main Street, Sedbergh
Telephone (015396) 20125

Local cycle hire

Arthur Caygill Cycles
Gallowfields Trading Estate, Richmond
Telephone (01748) 825469

Dave Ferguson Cycles
1 Brook Street, Skipton
Telephone (01756) 795367

Kettlewell Garage
Kettlewell
Telephone (01756) 760225

Stuart Price
Fremington
Telephone (01748) 826960

Sedbergh Cycle Hire
Old Ambulance Station, Sedbergh
Telephone (015396) 21000

Three Peaks Mountain Bikes
Horton-in-Ribblesdale
Telephone (01729) 860200

Local cycle shops

Arthur Caygill Cycles
Gallowfields Trading Estate, Richmond
Telephone (01748) 825469

G. Dawkins & Son
Bedale
Telephone (01677) 422491

Dave Ferguson Cycles
1 Brook Street, Skipton
Telephone (01756) 795367

Route 1

LEYBURN, WENSLEY AND MIDDLEHAM

Route information

Distance 13km (8 miles)

Grade Moderate

Terrain Two quiet main roads in and out of Leyburn. The rest of the route is over minor roads and an easy section of bridleway that can be tackled by most bicycles. One long and two shorter climbs.

Time to allow 1–3 hours.

Getting there by car Leyburn is in the north east of the Yorkshire Dales and can be reached on the A6108 or A684. There is parking in the town centre or in the signed long stay car park.

Getting there by train There is no practical railway access to this ride.

A short route, linking some great family attractions – out of Leyburn and downhill to Wensley and a candle workshop, from where the only serious climb of this route (easily walked) takes you south along a bridleway to the Forbidden Corner gardens and grotto. The route then heads east, past the scenic Coverham Bridge and into Middleham with its 12th-century castle. A quiet main road and a short climb take you back into Leyburn where there is the Tea Pottery and Violin Workshop.

Route description

From the Tourist Information Centre in the centre of Leyburn, cycle up the street towards the Bolton Arms. TL at TJ, SP Wensley/Aysgarth Falls/Hawes and cycle down the A684 towards Wensley. Continue through Wensley (passing the candle workshop) and over the River Ure.

1 TL, SP Coverdale, Carlton, for a steep climb. Pass the pillars of Spigot Lodge on the right.

2 At next right hand bend, TL (effectively SO) through gate SP Public Bridleway (5km/3 miles). Follow the firm track as it curves uphill to the right. Continue SO through the gate to Tupgill Park and through the stables. The entrance to the Forbidden Corner is on the right. TL in front of the entrance and follow the tarmac drive down to the main entrance of Tupgill Park, passing SP Birdridding/Deerclose.

3 At main entrance (TJ), TL, no SP, and continue on flat road. To visit Coverham Bridge, TR SP Caldbergh after 0.5km (0.3 mile), continue for a further 0.5km (0.3 mile). Otherwise continue. Climb a short, steep hill and cycle to Middleham, passing Middleham Low Moor on your left.

4 Arrive Middleham (9.5km/6 miles). Cycle through the town, passing the castle on the right.

5 TL at TJ onto A6108, SP Leyburn (the road is not usually busy). Cycle over bridge for a climb back into Leyburn.

6 TL at TJ, SP Hawes. Pass WC on right – TR here for 400m to visit the Tea Pottery and Violin Workshop. Otherwise continue into Leyburn, to the Tourist Information Centre and the end of the route. ***13km (8 miles)***

Places of interest along the route

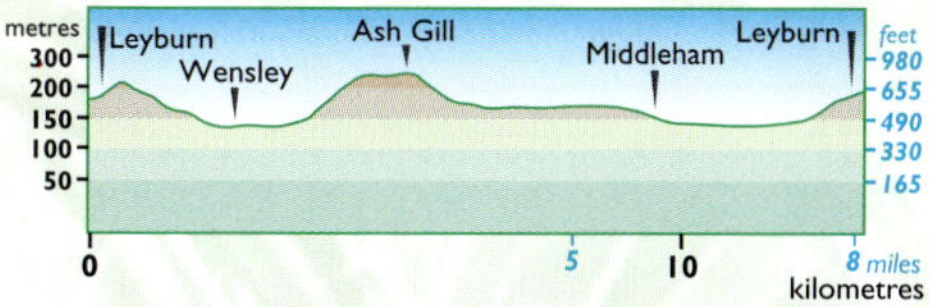

A Leyburn

Leyburn is an attractive old market town, with interesting shops and galleries, an antiques auction house and a market each Friday. It is a popular centre for visitors to Wensleydale. The **Tea Pottery**, a purpose-built pottery studio and showroom, produces nothing else but teapots – each one individually cast, hand-painted and decorated. A walkway through the studio, with informative printed panels, leads the visitor through each stage of manufacture. Gift shop;

cups of tea available. Studio and gift shop open all year, Monday–Friday 0900–1700; gift shop also open weekends, 0900–1700. Admission free. Telephone (01969) 623839. Also in Leyburn is the **Violin Workshop**. Violins have been made in the same way for hundreds of years and visitors to the workshop can discover how they are created, with lots on hands-on displays, workshop, viewing gallery and video presentation. Gift shop. Open from Easter to June and September, Sunday–Friday 1000–1700, Saturday 1200–1630; July–August, daily 1200–1630. Note no violin manufacture at weekends. Charge. Telephone (01969) 624416.

B White Rose Candle Workshop, Wensley

Located in a 19th-century watermill, the workshop manufactures candles of all types and visitors can see the various traditional dipping and casting methods involved. The gift shop stocks a comprehensive range of candles and candle holders. Scenic waterfall. Opening times vary between February and May (telephone for details); June to November, Sunday–Tuesday and Thursday–Friday 1000–1700 (or dusk if earlier); December usually open Sunday 1000–dusk. Telephone (01969) 623544 for further information.

C The Forbidden Corner, Tupgill Park Estate, Coverham

The Forbidden Corner is a grotto comprising gardens, woods, follies and an underground labyrinth of chambers and passages for visitors to explore. Shop and tearoom. Grotto and gardens open August, daily 1100–1700. Shop and tearoom open April to October, daily 1000–1700. Charge for grotto and garden but free admission to shop and tearoom.

D Coverham Bridge

As you ride through Coverham, a road to the right will take you the 0.5km (0.3 mile) to picturesque Coverham Bridge, on a beautiful part of the River Cover.

E Middleham

Middleham sits in lower Wensleydale, just outside the boundary of the Yorkshire Dales National Park, between the Rivers Cover and Ure. There is a thriving race horse industry in the town, with around 12 training stables – the number of horses stabled is said to equal half the town's population. The horses are trained on Middleham Low Moor, to the west of Middleham. The town itself is dominated by the ruins of **Middleham Castle**, the childhood home of Richard III. The massive 12th-century keep is one of the largest built in England and there are magnificent views from the battlements. English Heritage property. Gift shop and tearoom, picnics welcome. Open April to October, daily 1000–1800 (or dusk if earlier); November to March, Wednesday–Sunday 1000–1600. Charge. Telephone (01969) 623899.

Food and drink

There are numerous eateries in Leyburn and Middleham. Refreshments are available at the Forbidden Corner and Middleham Castle.

Castle Keep, Middleham

Cheerful tearoom and B&B in a 17th-century listed building, just in front of Middleham Castle.

Route 2

UPPER WENSLEYDALE – BAINBRIDGE TO HAWES

Route information

Distance 17km (10.5 miles)

Grade Moderate

Terrain The outward route follows gently undulating roads; on the return a steady climb leads to an off-road descent on a firm track, suitable for most types of bicycle.

Time to allow 2–3 hours.

Getting there by car Bainbridge is in Wensleydale, on the A684 Leyburn to Sedbergh road. There is car parking around the village green.

Getting there by train The closest railway station is at Garsdale on the Carlisle–Settle line, 10km (6 miles) from Hawes. Telephone (0345) 484950 for information.

A quiet minor road, giving lovely views down Wensleydale, takes you from Bainbridge into the bustling tourist town of Hawes. The route out of Hawes is initially flat and then climbs steadily up to an old Roman road, now a byway, leading to a glorious descent back into Bainbridge.

Places of interest along the route

A Bainbridge

Bainbridge is an attractive village that has retained its village green and stocks. The Romans arrived in this area circa AD 80 and built a succession of forts on nearby Brough Hill, to the east of the village. During the Middle Ages this part of Upper Wensleydale was covered by dense woodland and the village of Bainbridge was inhabited by foresters. Seven hundred years later the villagers of Bainbridge carry on a tradition originally started by those earlier inhabitants – each evening between the Feast of Holy Rood (September) and Shrovetide (early spring), a bull horn is blown to help guide the locals home. The River Bain is the shortest river in the country. It runs 3.5km (2 miles) between Semer Water, south west of Bainbridge, to the River Ure. As it passes through Bainbridge it powers the water wheel of the restored Bainbridge Low Mill. Telephone the Yorkshire Dales National Park Centre at Hawes on (01969) 667450 for further information.

B Hawes

Market towns are a particular feature of the Yorkshire Dales and Hawes is said to be the highest market town in England. Tuesday is market day and there are several craft workshops. The **Dales Countryside Museum**, housed in the old railway station, explains how the people of the Dales have influenced the evolution of the distinctive Dales landscape. There are exhibits on upland farming, domestic life in the early 20th century, wool and hand-knitting (once a major industry in the area), lead mining, stone cutting, dairying and cheese-making. Hands-on displays and a Time Tunnel, illustrating 10,000 years of Dales history. Gift shop. Open April to October, daily 1000–1700; limited winter opening – telephone for details. Charge. Telephone (01969) 667450. At the **Hawes Ropemakers**, located next to the Countryside Museum, visitors can see traditional ropemaking and learn how the many thin strands of yarn are rapidly twisted into strong rope. The ropeworks manufacture all manner of items, from skipping ropes and dog leads to church bell ropes. Gift shop. Open all year, Monday–Friday 0900–1730; July to October also open Saturday, 1000–1730. Free admission. Telephone (01969) 667487. The **Wensleydale Creamery** manufactures real Wensleydale cheese – there is a viewing gallery overlooking the manufacturing area, a museum explaining the history of Wensleydale cheese and a food hall. Guided tours, audio-video presentation, restaurant and coffee shop. The best time to see cheesemaking is between 1030 and 1500. Open all year, Monday–Saturday 0930–1700, Sunday 1000–1630. Charge. Telephone (01969) 667664.

Food and drink

Bainbridge has several pubs, a convenience store and a hotel which serves cream teas. There are numerous tearooms and pubs in Hawes and refreshments are available at the Wensleydale Creamery.

Rose & Crown, Bainbridge

Village pub serving bar meals at lunchtimes and in the evenings.

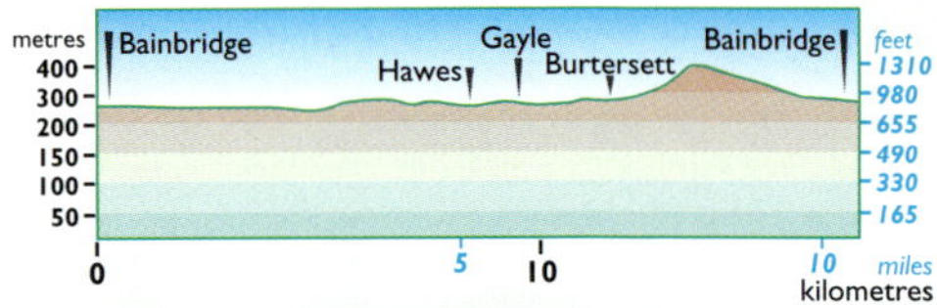

Near Hawes, Wensleydale

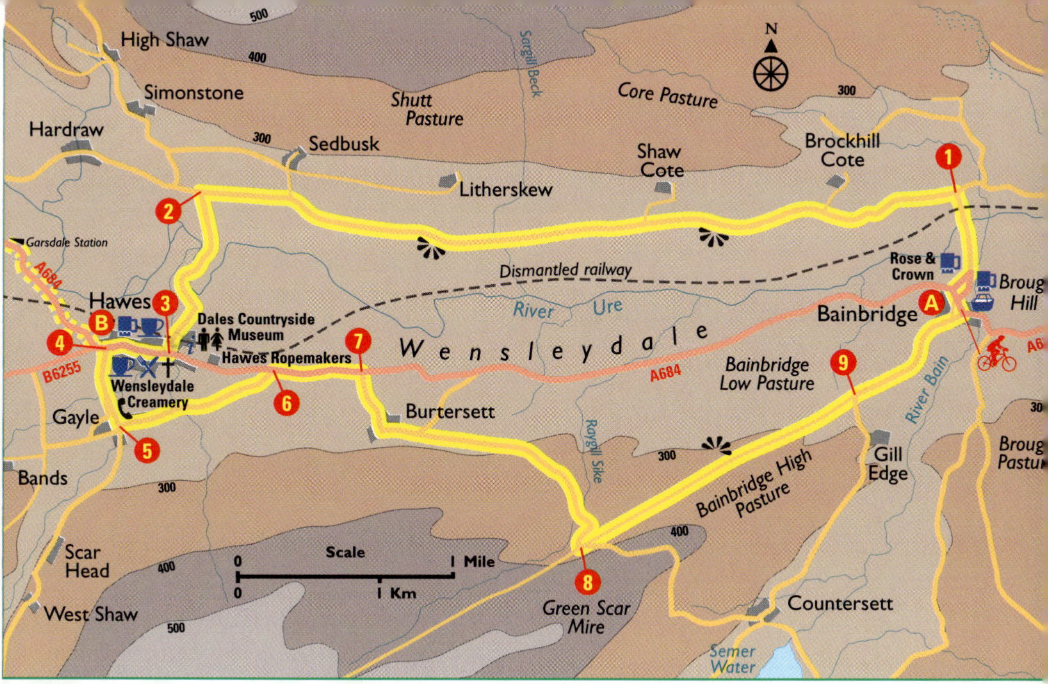

Route description

If starting this route from Garsdale Station, leave the station and follow the A684 into Hawes where TR, SP Gayle/Kettlewell (at direction 4). Continue through Gayle, passing Wensleydale Creamery on the left and continue to direction 5.

Otherwise, from the Post Office/village shop in Bainbridge, head towards the Rose & Crown pub (with the village green to your left). Follow the one-way system and TR at TJ, SP Aysgarth/Leyburn/ Askrigg. Almost immediately TL, SP Askrigg.

1 TL at TJ, SP Hardraw/Hawes. Cycle the undulating, quiet minor road with great views along Wensleydale.

2 TL, SP Hawes (6.5km/4 miles). Descend and cross bridge.

3 SO at XR, SP Sedbergh/Ingleton. Then immediately TR and follow the one-way system or visit the Dales Countryside Museum and the Ropemaker on the left of this junction. Continue along cobbled streets, passing the church on the left. The one way system finishes at the end of the cobbles.

4 TL, SP Gayle/Kettlewell (SP on left), and enter Gayle. Pass Wensleydale Creamery on the left.

5 TL, SP Bainbridge.

6 TR at TJ onto A684, no SP (10km/6miles). Seat and Hawes SP on left. Continue along A684.

7 TR, SP Burtersett. Cycle uphill, through the village, and bear right, SP Countersett. Continue the steady climb, crossing a bridge over a waterfall.

8 Soon after the bridge TL at XR, SP Byway Bainbridge 2ML (this TL is easy to miss – the wide byway crosses the road at this point and there is a red arrow on the SP). Follow this old Roman road as it steadily descends.

9 TL at TJ onto tarmac, no SP (16km/ 10 miles). Descend quickly into Bainbridge where TR, SP Aysgarth/Leyburn to complete the route. ***17km (10.5 miles)***

If returning to Garsdale Station, continue the route from the Post Office/village shop. At direction 4, SO then TR back onto A684 and continue to Garsdale Station.

Route 3

AYSGARTH FALLS AND ASKRIGG

Route information

Distance 18km (11 miles)

Grade Easy

Terrain Quiet minor roads and a short section of A road through Aysgarth. One steep climb.

Time to allow 2–3 hours.

Getting there by car Aysgarth is on the A684 Leyburn to Sedbergh road. SP for car park in Aysgarth – follow the road downhill past the falls, over the bridge and the car park entrance is on the left.

Getting there by train There is no practical railway access to this ride.

This route climbs out of Aysgarth and heads west to Askrigg, with good views along Wensleydale. Out of Askrigg, the route crosses the River Ure for a steep climb to the hamlet of Cubeck. The reward is an extremely quiet ride back to Aysgarth, along a tree-lined road.

Route description

From the National Park Centre, north of Aysgarth, TL uphill and immediately pass under an old railway bridge. Continue north towards Carperby.

1 TL at TJ, SP Askrigg/Hawes. Cycle along the flat two-laned road west towards Askrigg.

2 Descend into Askrigg. Pass the Crown Inn on the right and arrive at the village centre. Leave village and return back up the hill, retracing the way you came in. TR, SP Worton (9km/5.5 miles). Descend and cross bridge over River Ure.

3 TL at TJ, no SP (telephone at right of junction). Immediately TR, SP Cubeck/Thornton Rust, for a short uphill climb. Continue through Cubeck and Thornton Rust and along the quiet, tree-lined road to Aysgarth.

4 In Aysgarth, TR at TJ onto A684, no SP.

16km (10 miles)

5 TL, SP Aysgarth Falls/Carperby/Bolton Castle/Redmire (youth hostel to right of junction). Steep descent (25%) to the end of the route, passing the Yorkshire Carriage Museum on the right, just before the bridge.

18km (11 miles)

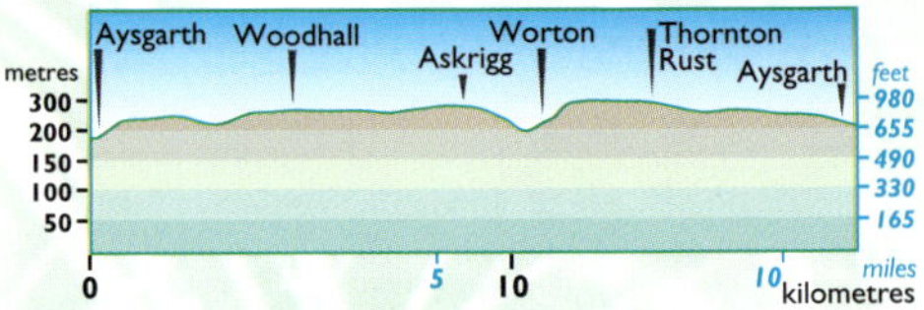

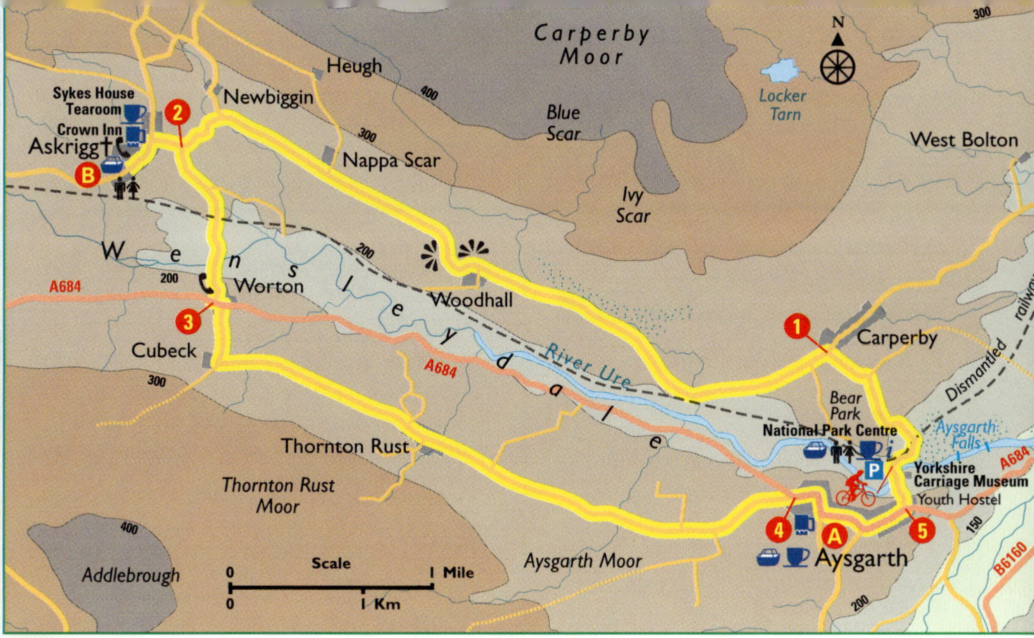

Places of interest along the route

Ⓐ Aysgarth

The River Ure flows through Aysgarth and, beside a 16th-century bridge, flows over a series of flat limestone blocks – **Aysgarth Falls**. The falls will be at their most spectacular after heavy rain, but are magnificent at any time. Admission by honesty box. For more information, telephone the National Park Centre in Aysgarth on (01969) 663424. The **Yorkshire Carriage Museum** is housed in a 200-year-old mill overlooking the Aysgarth Falls. There are 57 genuine Victorian carriages on display together with collections of postcards of horsedrawn carriages and hand-made scale models. Open March to October, daily 0930–dusk; November to February, daily 1200–dusk. Telephone (01969) 663399.

Ⓑ Askrigg

Pretty Dales village of 17th- and 18th-century houses. The 15th-century church of St Oswald is the largest church in Wensleydale. Askrigg was once a centre of hand-knitting and clock-making. For further information, telephone the Aysgarth National Park Centre on (01969) 663424

Food and drink

There are several pubs, tearooms and convenience stores in Aysgarth and Askrigg, and a tearoom at the National Park Centre in Aysgarth.

Sykes House Tearoom, Askrigg
Teas, coffees and snacks.

Route 4

SETTLE AND THE SOUTHERN DALES

Route information

Distance 20km (12.5 miles)

Grade Moderate

Terrain Quiet lanes throughout, with steady climbs and descents. There is one short steep climb near the end of the route.

Time to allow 1–3 hours.

Getting there by car Settle is on the south western edge of the Yorkshire Dales National Park, just north of the A65. There is a long stay car park in the town.

Getting there by train Settle is on the Carlisle–Settle line. Telephone (0345) 484950 for information.

From Settle, a steady climb north along a quiet lane leading to a descent into Austwick. From there the route goes out towards Lawkland, with an optional detour to the Yorkshire Dales Falconry & Conservation Centre. An undulating lane and a steep but short climb provide a good descent back to Settle.

Route description

TR out of Settle Station, into Station Road, SP Town Centre. TL at TJ opposite the police station and cycle through the town centre. Pass under railway bridge and cross the River Ribble into Giggleswick.

1 TR, SP Stackhouse/Little Stainforth, and climb steadily up the valley to reach open moorland and a descent.

2 TL at XR opposite quarry entrance, no SP (6.5km/4 miles). Continue along a walled, gently undulating road, punctuated by stone barns. Take care on the descent towards Austwick, as there can be strong crosswinds here. Arrive Austwick.

3 TL at TJ by the village green, SP Settle (11km/7 miles). Cycle out of the village, passing seats and crossing a bridge.

4 SO at XR, SP Lawkland, and enter the Yorkshire Dales National Park.

5 To visit the Falconry & Conservation Centre, take first TL and cycle for 1km (0.6 mile) along a flat road. Retrace your route and TL. Otherwise, continue along a windy, undulating hedged lane towards Giggleswick.

6 TL at XR, SP Giggleswick. Climb towards A65. ***16km (10 miles)***

7 SO at staggered XR, across the A65 with care. (There is good visibility either side of this junction, and wide grass verges – it is probably best to walk across.) Continue with a short, steep climb and then a descent into Giggleswick to the bottom of the hill, passing a school on the right.

8 TR, no SP. Cross a bridge, pass church on left and post office and stores on right.

9 Just after the post office, TL up a short hill, no SP. TR at TJ at the top, SP Settle. Keep to this road back into town and to Settle Station. ***20km (12.5 miles)***

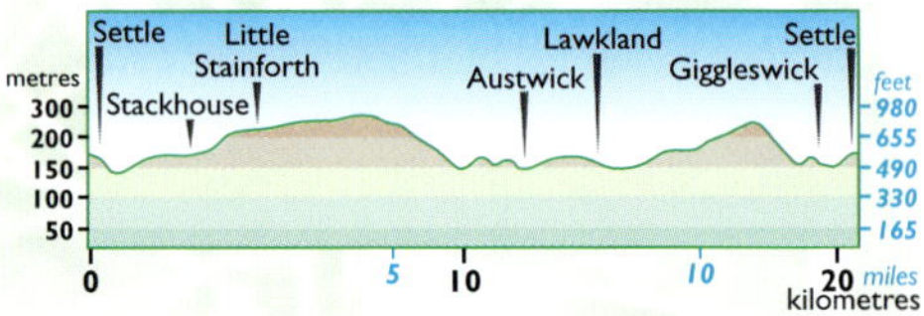

Food and drink

Settle has numerous places for refreshment, and there is a tearoom at the Falconry & Conservation Centre. There is a convenience store in Austwick and in Giggleswick close to the end of the route.

The Game Cock, Austwick
Pub with small beamed snug, conservatory and picnic tables outside. Bar meals available. Closed Wednesdays.

Cross Streets Inn, near Austwick
Bar meals served.

Places of interest along the route

A Settle

The southern Dales are a mix of remote fells and gritstone moors, limestone cliffs and gorges, and lush pastures and valleys. Settle, one of the Dales' many attractive market towns, sits amongst this splendour, beside the largest outcrop of limestone in Britain, an area of caves, cliffs and potholes. It is also on the Carlisle–Settle railway – the country's most arduous railway line with a gradient of 1 in 100. The line was constructed between 1869 and 1876 and still runs a regular passenger service, with occasional special services of steam trains. Market day is Tuesday, and the market square, flanked by interesting 17th- and 18th-century buildings and the Shambles, is where the butchers were originally sited. The **Watershed Mill Visitor Centre**, on the B6479/Langcliffe Road, is housed in an 1820s cotton mill, beside the River Ribble. The centre is an outlet for Dales-made local crafts – woodwork, pottery, leatherwork, paintings, prints and textiles. Craft demonstrations are held regularly. There is also a rock and fossil shop and a coffee shop. Open all year, Monday–Saturday 1000–1730, Sunday 1100–1730. Admission free. Telephone (01729) 825539 for information.

B Yorkshire Dales Falconry & Conservation Centre, near Giggleswick

The centre is home to many species of birds of prey from around the world – eagles, hawks, vultures, falcons and owls – many of them endangered species. The birds are housed in specially created aviaries, as close to their natural habitat as possible. Flying demonstrations are held at regular times throughout the day. Visitors, who are encouraged to take part in the demonstrations, can see the largest bird in the world, the Andean Condor, in free flight, together with a Griffon Vulture, falcons and owls. Gift shop and tearoom. Open most days throughout the year, 1000–dusk. Flying demonstrations take place at 1200, 1330, 1500 and 1630 each day. Charge. Telephone (01792) 825164 to check opening times or (01792) 822832 for further information.

Dry stone walls, southern Dales

Route 5

PATELEY BRIDGE AND NIDDERDALE

Route information

Distance 22km (13.5 miles)

Grade Moderate

Terrain Moderate to flat riding; two lovely sections of off-road along firm tracks, suitable for most types of bicycle.

Time to allow 2–3 hours.

Getting there by car Pateley Bridge is in the southern Dales, on the B6265 Ripon to Grassington road. Car parking is available in the Nidd Street long stay car park, on the B6265 near the bridge.

Getting there by train There is no practical railway access to this ride.

This route takes you through beautiful Nidderdale. From Pateley Bridge the route heads north, along a quiet minor road to Wath, from where a scenic bridleway takes you down to Gouthwaite Reservoir and along its eastern shore. On through Ramsgill to How Stean Gorge and the second bridleway, before rejoining the road to Pateley Bridge.

Places of interest along the route

A Nidderdale Museum, Pateley Bridge

Nidderdale, the valley of the River Nidd, stretches from Ripley in the south east, to the river's source in the north west, on Great Whernside. The award-winning Nidderdale Museum illustrates all aspects of local life and history. Displays include, among others, a cobbler's shop, general store, Victorian parlour, kitchen and schoolroom. There are exhibitions on agriculture, religion, industries, transport and costume. Open April to September, daily 1400–1700; October to March, Sunday only 1400–1700. Charge. Telephone (01423) 711225 for information.

B Gouthwaite Reservoir

The reservoir is home to a wide variety of birds – Canada geese, herons, waders and, in winter, birds of prey such as goshawks and peregrine falcons. Watch the birds from the bridleway or from specially built hides. For further information, telephone the Tourist Information Centre at Pateley Bridge on (01423) 711147.

C How Stean Gorge, near Pateley Bridge

A spectacular limestone gorge with a deep-sided ravine, 24m (80 feet) deep in places. The sides of the ravine support a wide variety of plants and wildlife. Visitors can walk through the gorge via footpaths and bridges spanning the ravine. Also two caves – How Stean Tunnel and Tom Taylor's Cave, named after a highwayman who reputedly hid here. Torches are needed to visit the caves and are available for hire. Tearoom. Open all year, daily 1000–1800. Charge. Telephone (01423) 755666.

Food and drink

Pateley Bridge has plenty of pubs and tearooms. The tearoom at How Stean Gorge serves typical cyclists' fare such as toasted teacakes.

Yorke Arms, Ramsgill

A pub and hotel. Bar and restaurant. Teas and coffees served.

Watermill Inn, Foster Beck

Pub and hotel in an 18th-century mill with restored water wheel. Inside, beams and open fires. Meals served all day, every day. Outside seating.

Route description

From the entrance of Nidd Street long stay car park, cross the B6265 at the XR and cycle along Long Street. There are shops either side as the road bends to the right, before a steep climb towards the church. Pass Nidderdale Museum on your left. Continue up the hill out of Pateley Bridge. Admire the view of Nidderdale from the top of the hill. Continue along this road to Wath.

1 As the road bends to the left, cross a small bridge over a stream on your right. Then, TR onto a track and pass SP Private Road (this **is** a bridleway, however). If you pass a telephone box on the right, you have gone too far. Continue up this steep hill through woodland. At the summit, leave the wood and bear left. Continue and cross a substantial bridge by a waterfall. Descend to the edge of the reservoir and follow the track towards Ramsgill, passing through several gates. Once Ramsgill comes into view, pass a farm to the right and continue on a wider track.

2 TL at TJ onto tarmac, no SP (7.5km/4.5 miles). Cycle downhill, passing a church on the right, and cross a bridge.

3 TR at TJ, SP Lofthouse/Middlesmoor (TL here to access Ramsgill). Continue into Lofthouse, where bear left, SP How Stean Gorge.

4 TL, SP How Stean Gorge, across bridge, bear right and climb. How Stean Gorge is on your right. After visiting the gorge, return down the hill. ***10km (6 miles)***

5 TR (effectively SO) just before the road swings left to cross the bridge. Go over a speed bump and bear right in front of the caravan site entrance. Pass farm buildings and TR up a cobbled track. When this track becomes tarmac, TL SP Public Bridleway Ramsgill/Nidderdale Way. Follow the track (grassy near the start) along the edge of the valley, passing through several gates, to the left of a farm and finally over several cattle grids back to Ramsgill.

6 TR at TJ in Ramsgill, no SP. Cycle along the western side of Gouthwaite Reservoir and on into Pateley Bridge (access to bird hides in Gouthwaite Reservoir car park).

7 TL at TJ, SP Ripon/Harrogate. (There is a small selection of bicycle spares in the garage to the right.) (21km/13 miles). Cross the bridge.

8 TR into Nidd Street car park to finish the route. ***22km (13.5 miles)***

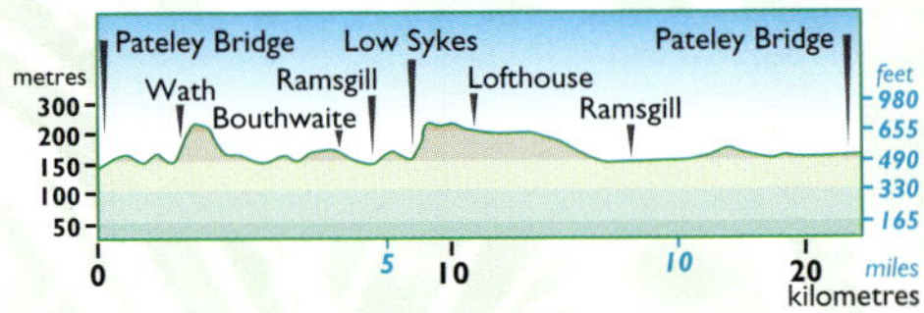

Northside Head
Ruscoe
Middlesmoor
Hazel Close
How Stean Gorge
Stean
Nidderdale
High Lofthouse
Lofthouse
High Ash Head Moor
Coverdale
Kirkby Malzeard Moor
Carle Moor
Sype Land
Hambleton Hill
Low Sykes
Nidderdale Way
Blayshaw Gill
Ramsgill Bents
East Side Wood
Helks
Lul Beck
Fountains Earth Moor
North Gill Beck
Dallowgill Moor
Ramsgill
Bouthwaite
Yorke Arms
Coville House Farm
Sigsworth Moor
Ramsgill Moor
Ramsgill Beck
Swine Beck Knotts
Sigsworth Crags
Moss Wood
Raygill House Moor
Riddingsgill Wood
Gouthwaite Reservoir
Dauber Gill
Colt House Gill
Gouthwaite Moor
Colt Plain
Carle Edge
Burn Gill Head Moss
Burn Gill
Cow Close Wood
High Ruckles
West Wood
Wath
High Bishop Side
Heathfield Moor
Heathfield
Highfield
Ashfold Side Beck
Low Green
Brownstay Ridge
Goose Green
Merryfield
Watermill Inn
Pateley Bridge
Blazerfield
Cross Gill Moor
Nidderdale Museum
Hardcastle
Brandstone Beck
Knott Side
Hardcastle Moor
Jack Hole Moss
Bewerley Moor
B6265
Bewerley
River Nidd
Scale
Mile
Km
Keld Houses
Greenhow Hill
Glasshouses

Route 6

GRASSINGTON AND UPPER WHARFEDALE

Route information

Distance 25.5km (16 miles)

Grade Moderate

Terrain A hard climb to begin with, followed by firm off-road tracks and quiet minor roads.

Time to allow 2–3 hours.

Getting there by car Grassington is in Wharfedale in the southern Dales, and can be reached on the B6265 from Skipton or Pateley Bridge, and the B6160 from Bolton Abbey. There is long term car parking at the well-signed National Park/Tourist Information Centre on the eastern side of the town.

Getting there by train There is no practical railway access to this route.

Starting from Grassington, this route heads west to Threshfield. From here, a steep climb leads to open countryside and a series of delightful byways and bridleways, with extensive views all around. Then downhill to a track leading to Cracoe. An undulating and quiet lane, with excellent views over Grassington village, completes the route.

Route description

TL out of the National Park/Tourist Information Centre and cycle towards the village. Follow the road round to the left, SP Skipton, and descend, crossing the River Wharfe.

1 TR at TJ, SP Kettlewell. Pass a garage on the left.

2 TL along Skirethorns Lane, SP Skirethorns. Follow the lane to the right, SP Malham/Unsuitable for Motor Vehicles, and start to climb. At the top, pass through a gate leading to Bordley Green Farm for a fast descent.

3 TL at XR (of byways), SP BW–Bordley (6.5km/4 miles). Descend into farm and pass Bordley House Farmhouse on the right.

4 Almost immediately after farmhouse, before entering main farmyard, TL, SP BW–Boss Moor. Pass through a small yard and onto a grassy lane that dips, climbs briefly and then gloriously descends again on a firm track. Pass a farm on the left and a telephone on the right (9km/5.5 miles). Then, a short steep climb leads to another long, fast descent on a tarmac road.

5 TR at TJ, no SP. ***14.5km (9 miles)***

6 TL, SP Rylstone/Skipton. Pass under a railway bridge.

7 TL at TJ, SP Cracoe/Grassington. Then immediately TR, SP Rylstone Church/Manor House Farm. Take great care on this road – it is used by quarry lorries. Follow the road past the church on the left and pass through a gate, SP Cracoe/C27C. Continue through a field (passing

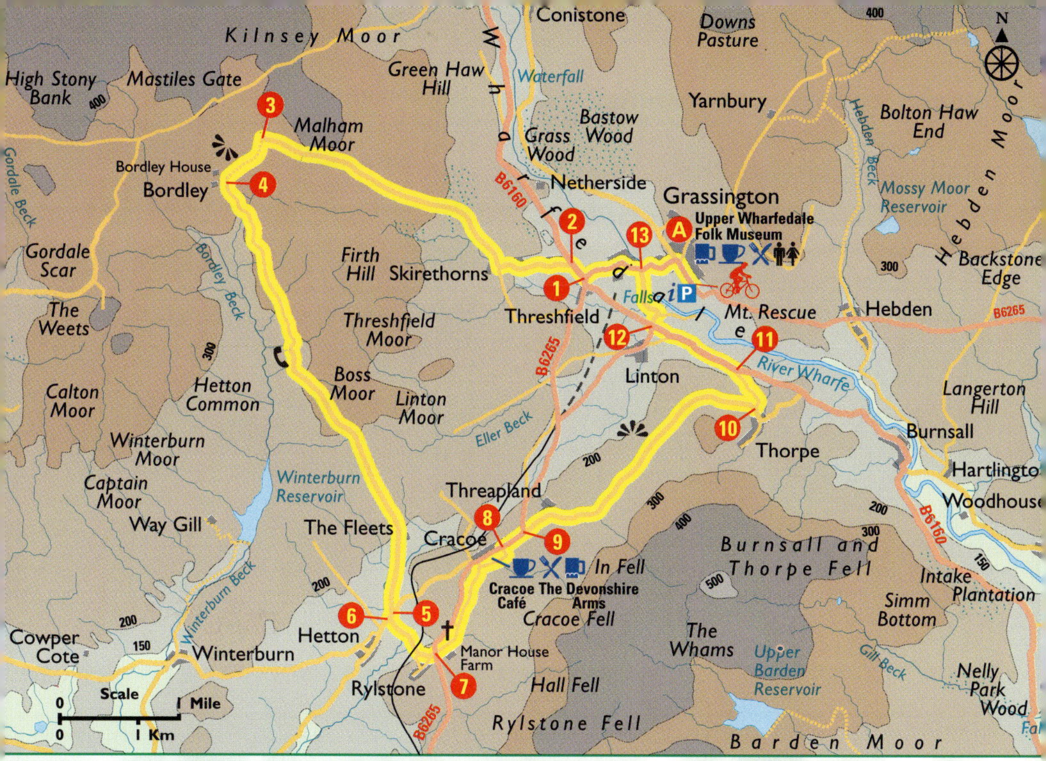

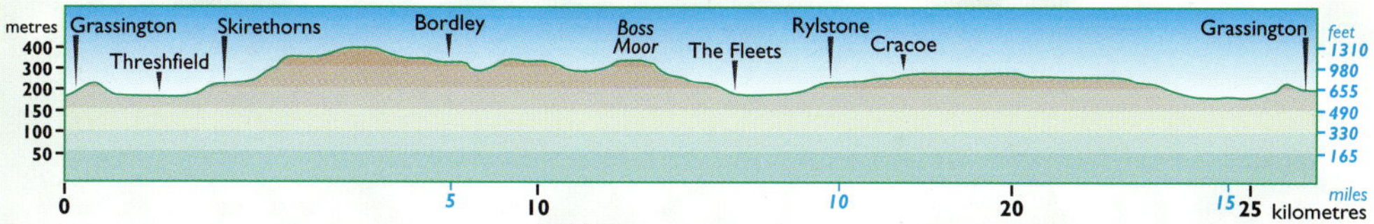

empty medieval fish ponds on the right) to the start of a track at the top left corner. Follow this track parallel to the adjacent B road. Just before the track meets the B road, TR onto a lane leading around the back of Cracoe. TL at TJ in front of the National Park information board.

8 TR at TJ onto B6265, no SP. (TL here for the Cracoe Café and the Devonshire Arms.)

9 TR (effectively SO), as the B road bears left (18km/11 miles). Pass a width restriction sign and climb.

10 TL at TJ, no SP. Descend.

22km (13.5 miles)

11 TL at TJ (opposite iron railings), no SP. Continue along Wharfedale.

12 TR at XR, SP Linton Falls. Descend and pass school on left.

13 TR at TJ, SP Grassington/Pateley Bridge. Cross River Wharfe and climb. Follow the road to the right and return to the National Park/Tourist Information Centre and the end of the ride. ***25.5km (16 miles)***

Places of interest along the route

Ⓐ Upper Wharfedale Folk Museum, Grassington
Grassington is a picturesque small town. The Folk Museum is located in two 18th-century lead miners' cottages in the town square and depicts the life and history of Upper Wharfedale. There are exhibits on lead mining, minerals, tools, farming, period costumes, folklore, the railway and World War II memorabilia. Open April to September, daily 1400–1630; October to March, Saturday and Sunday 1400–1630. Nominal charge. For further information, telephone Grassington National Park/Tourist Information Centre on (01756) 752774.

Food and drink

There are many opportunities for refreshment in Grassington.

Cracoe Café, Cracoe
A typical Dales café – tea, coffee and good food.

The Devonshire Arms, Cracoe
On the Bolton Abbey Estate, owned by the Duke and Duchess of Devonshire. The hotel is furnished with antiques and paintings from Chatsworth House. Restaurant and bar.

River Wharfe

Route 7

SKIPTON AND BOLTON ABBEY

Route information

Distance 26km (16 miles)

Grade Moderate.

Terrain A short section of A road in and out of Skipton, otherwise undulating quiet lanes.

Time to allow 2–4 hours.

Getting there by car Skipton is on the southern edge of the Yorkshire Dales, reached via the A59, A65 and A629. There is long term car parking in the town.

Getting there by train There is a regular service to Skipton Station. Telephone (0345) 484950 for information.

From Skipton a short stretch of upward A road leads towards Embsay. From here the route follows a quiet lane to the Bolton Abbey Estate and the quieter side of Wharfedale, before climbing over Halton Moor for a descent back to Skipton.

Places of interest along the route

A Skipton

Skipton is a popular centre for touring the Yorkshire Dales, with cobbled streets and alleyways. The 12th-century **Skipton Castle** is one of the best-preserved medieval castles in England, despite being at the centre of a three-year siege during the Civil War. Illustrated tour sheet, picnic area and gift shop. Open March to September, Monday–Saturday 1000–1800, Sunday 1400–1800; October to February, Monday–Saturday 1000–1600; Sunday 1400–1600. Charge. Telephone (01756) 792442. The **Craven Museum** is situated on the first floor of Skipton Town Hall and features the history and character of Skipton and the local dales. Exhibits on rocks and minerals, pre-historic and Roman history, Victorian homes and much other local history. Open April to September, Monday and Wednesday–Saturday 1000–1700, Sunday 1400–1700; October to March, Monday and Wednesday–Friday 1330–1700, Saturday 1000–1700. Admission free. Telephone (01756) 706407.

B Embsay and Bolton Steam Railway, Embsay

The Embsay and Bolton Steam Railway runs regular services along a picturesque line to Bolton Abbey Station, 3km (2 miles) from Bolton Abbey village. Café and picnic area, gift and book shop, buffet cars. Bicycles are carried (telephone to pre-book). Steam trains run every Sunday throughout the year; Tuesday, Saturday and Sunday from June to mid-July; Tuesday–Thursday, Saturday and Sunday from mid-July to end August; also on Bank Holidays. Charge. Speaking timetable (01756) 795189; general enquiries (01756) 794727.

C Bolton Abbey Estate, near Skipton

Bolton Abbey Estate is the Yorkshire estate of the Duke and Duchess of Devonshire. It comprises moorland and woodland, many miles of footpaths and nature trails. The River Wharfe runs through the estate and is famous for its trout fishing and wildlife. Overlooking the river are the imposing

Bolton Priory

ruins of a 12th-century **priory** and a restored and thriving parish church. Strid Wood sits alongside the river, close to the Strid, a spectacular point where the river surges through a narrow gorge. Further along the valley are also the ruins of the impressive 15th-century shooting lodge, **Barden Tower**. The estate is open all year but the opening times of the various teashops and restaurants should be confirmed by telephone. Admission free. Telephone (01756) 710533.

Route description

From the Tourist Information Centre in Skipton, cycle up the street, past the Craven Museum, towards the church. TR at the roundabout in front of the church, SP Embsay/Bolton Abbey. Continue out of Skipton, passing Skipton Castle on the left.

1 TL, SP Embsay, and cycle into Embsay, passing the Embsay and Bolton Steam Railway on the right. You can catch a train from here to Bolton Abbey Station, where TL and cycle into Bolton Abbey village, going SO at direction 4.

2 TR into Shires Lane, SP Halton East/Bolton Abbey.

3 TR at TJ into Low Lane, SP Halton East/ Bolton Abbey (3.5km/2 miles). Continue through Halton East to Bolton Abbey.

4 TL at TJ, no SP, and pass under a distinctive arch. ***10.5km (6.5 miles)***

5 TR by the fountain monument, no SP. Descend towards the Cavendish Pavilion and walk across the footbridge over the River Wharfe.

6 TL at TJ opposite Bolton Park Farm, no SP. Cycle along this undulating, narrow road towards Barden.

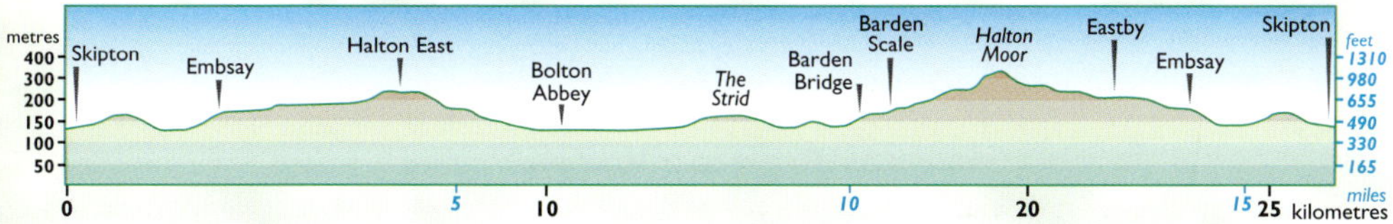

7 TL (sharp turn) at TJ, no SP. Arrive Barden. ***15.5km (9.5 miles)***

8 TL at TJ onto B6160, SP Bolton Abbey. Pass Barden Tower on the left.

9 TR, SP Embsay/Dales Railway. Climb to a good view and descend, taking care on the 14% descent. Enter Eastby.

10 TR at TJ, SP Skipton (22.5km/14 miles). Pass the Methodist Church on the right, after which the road bends left then right, passing pubs and a convenience store, and (after bends) the Embsay and Bolton Steam Railway. Continue towards Skipton.

11 TR at TJ onto the A6131, SP Skipton. Continue into Skipton, TL at the roundabout and cycle back to the Tourist Information Centre and the end of the route. ***26km (16 miles)***

Food and drink

There are a variety of eating places in Skipton, three pubs and a convenience store in Embsay, and a convenience store and tearoom in Bolton Abbey village.

Cavendish Pavilion, Bolton Abbey Estate
A large purpose built café at the entrance to Strid Wood. Also gift shop and displays on the estate and Strid Woods.

Barden Tower Tearoom, Bolton Abbey Estate
Located in a 15th-century priests house, adjacent to Barden Tower.

Route 8

WEST TANFIELD – THE EDGE OF THE DALES

Route information

Distance 27km (17 miles)

Grade Easy

Terrain Minor roads throughout.

Time to allow 2–3 hours.

Getting there by car West Tanfield is on the A6108, Leyburn to Ripon road. There is free car parking in the centre of the village, close to the start of the route.

Getting there by train There is no practical rail access to this route.

A flexible route – cycle it all and visit the places of interest (31.5km/19.5 miles), keeping to the route itself, or use the short cut half-way through the ride to reduce the distance to approximately 13km (8 miles). A quiet lane leads from West Tanfield to Wath, where an optional 1km (0.6 mile) diversion goes to Norton Conyers, an interesting old house and garden. The route turns north, through Sutton Howgrave where the village green invites a picnic. Onto Kirklington and Carthorpe, after which a quiet road leads to Snape. Another optional side trip of 1km (0.6 mile) takes in Thorp Perrow Arboretum, before the route heads south back to West Tanfield.

Places of interest along the route

A Marmian Tower, West Tanfield

An English Heritage property, Marmian Tower is the 14th-century gatehouse of the former Tanfield Castle. Access at all reasonable times. Free. For further information telephone English Heritage on 0171-973 3434.

B Norton Conyers, near Ripon

A charming old house and walled garden. The house was constructed during medieval times and was altered during the Stuart reign and again in the 18th century. The Graham family has lived in the house since 1624, and this long tenure is reflected in the pictures and furniture. Charles I visited the house in 1632 and James II in 1679. Charlotte Bronte also stayed in the house, in 1839, and Norton Conyers is believed to be the original Thornfield Hall from her classic *Jane Eyre*. Family wedding dresses and other costumes are also on display. Parkland and 18th-century walled garden with orangery, yew hedges and herbaceous border. House open 1400–1700, June to September, Sunday and Bank Holiday Mondays; garden open 1130–1700, days as above. The house and garden are usually open daily for a week in July. Pick-your-own fruit (raspberries, red currants and gooseberries) in season. Charge. To confirm opening, telephone (01765) 640333.

Marmian Tower, West Tanfield

C Thorp Perrow Arboretum, near Bedale

Thorp Perrow was the creation of Colonel Sir Leonard Ropner (1895–1977) and is now managed by Sir John Ropner. The 34ha (85 acre) arboretum is set in over 405ha (1000 acres) of parkland. The collection of trees comes from around the world and contains the national collections of oak, ash, lime and walnut. There are numerous other species – some of the rarest and largest trees and shrubs in the country. Woodland walks, nature trail, lake, picnic area, tearoom and plant sales. Open all year, dawn to dusk. Charge. Telephone (01677) 425323.

Food and drink

There are pubs in the villages throughout the route – at Wath, Kirklington, Carthorpe and Well – as well as a tearoom at Thorp Perrow Arboretum. There is a shop in West Tanfield.

Black Bull, West Tanfield

Village pub serving meals, teas and coffees.

Route description

From the roundabout in the centre of West Tanfield, head east, passing the the village shop on the left and tennis courts on the right. Follow SP for Wath along a flat, hedged lane.

1 To visit Norton Conyers, TR at TJ and continue for 1km (0.6 mile). After your visit, retrace to this junction and SO to direction 2. Otherwise, TL at TJ, SP Melmerby/Thirsk.

2 TL, SP Sutton Howgrave/Bedale.

6.5km (4 miles)

3 TL, SP Sutton Howgrave. Enter the village and bear right past the village green.

4 TL at TJ, SP Kirklington/Thirsk/Bedale.

10km (6 miles)

5 If you want to take the short cut, TL SP Masham and continue to Nosterfield.

a TL, no SP (just before Freemason's Arms) and continue for 1km (0.6 mile).

b TR at TJ next to Nosterfield Nature Reserve, no SP.

c TR at TJ, SP West Tanfield and continue back into village.

Otherwise, to continue route, SO at XR, SP Kirklington/Bedale, and continue to Kirklington.

6 TL at TJ, SP Carthorpe/Bedale, and continue to Carthorpe.

7 In Carthorpe, TL, SP Snape/Tanfield (14.5km/9 miles). Continue through Snape.

8 To visit the arboretum, TR at TJ and continue for 1km (0.6 mile). After visiting, retrace your route to this junction where SO to direction 9.

To continue route, TL at TJ, SP Well/West Tanfield (21km/13 miles), and continue to Well.

9 SO at XR, SP Tanfield/Ripon. Cycle back into West Tanfield to complete the route.

27km (17 miles)

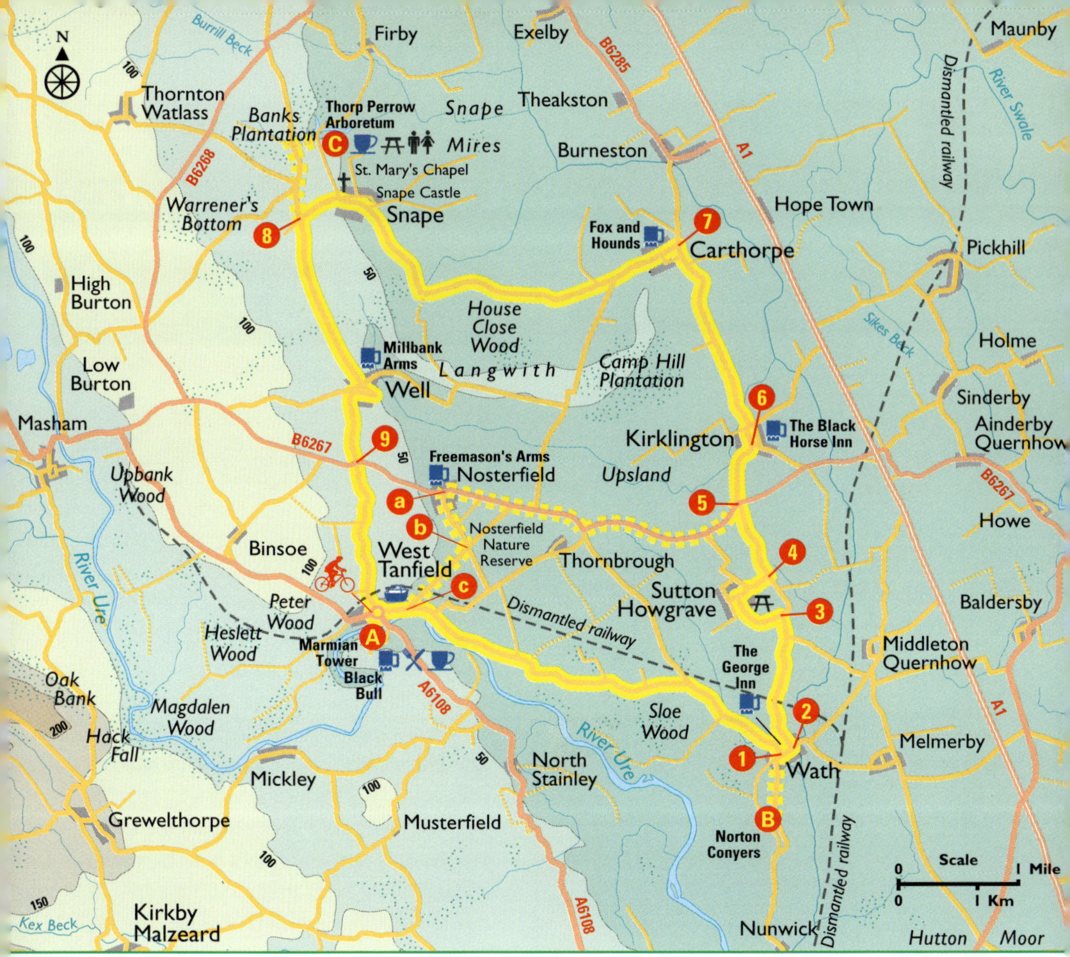
N
Burrill Beck
Firby
Exelby
B6285
Maunby
Thornton Watlass
Banks Plantation
Thorp Perrow Arboretum
C
Snape
Mires
Theakston
Burneston
A1
Dismantled railway
River Swale
St. Mary's Chapel
Snape Castle
Snape
B6268
Warrener's Bottom
8
Hope Town
Fox and Hounds
7
Carthorpe
Pickhill
High Burton
House Close Wood
Low Burton
Millbank Arms
Langwith
Camp Hill Plantation
Sikes Beck
Holme
Well
6
Sinderby
Masham
B6267
9
Kirklington
The Black Horse Inn
Ainderby Quernhow
Freemason's Arms
Nosterfield
Upsland
Upbank Wood
a
5
B6267
Howe
b
Nosterfield Nature Reserve
Binsoe
West Tanfield
Thornbrough
4
River Ure
Sutton Howgrave
c
Baldersby
Peter Wood
3
Heslett Wood
Dismantled railway
A
Marmian Tower
Middleton Quernhow
The George Inn
Black Bull
Oak Bank
A6108
Sloe Wood
2
Magdalen Wood
A1
Hack Fall
River Ure
Melmerby
1
Wath
North Stainley
Mickley
Grewelthorpe
Musterfield
B
Norton Conyers
Dismantled railway
Scale
0
1 Mile
0
1 Km
Kirkby Malzeard
Kex Beck
A6108
Nunwick
Hutton Moor

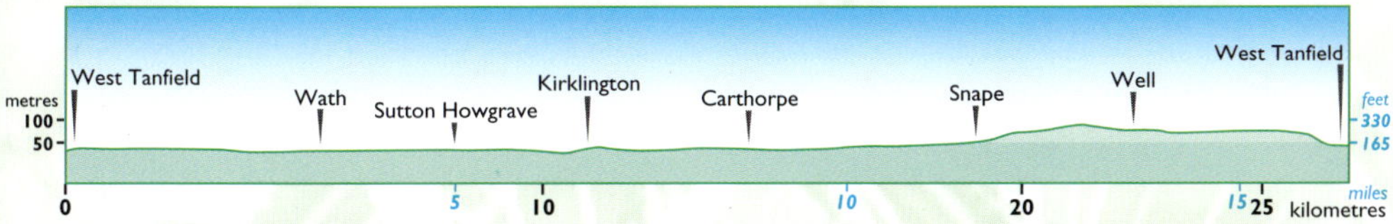
West Tanfield
Wath
Sutton Howgrave
Kirklington
Carthorpe
Snape
Well
West Tanfield
metres
100
50
feet
330
165
0
5
10
10
20
15
25
miles
kilometres

Route 9

BARNARD CASTLE AND EGGLESTONE ABBEY

Route information

Distance 28km (17.5 miles)

Grade Moderate

Terrain Mostly quiet, undulating lanes. There is one climb into Barningham, and a short (1km/0.6 mile) section along the A66, half of which is along a slip road – please take care.

Time to allow 2–3 hours.

Getting there by car Barnard Castle is on the northern edge of the Dales, on the A67 (off the A66 Appleby to Darlington road). There is a free long term car park (signed) near the centre of town.

Getting there by train There is no practical rail access to this route.

This route heads south east from Barnard Castle, initially following the River Tees, past the ruins of Egglestone Abbey. Great care is needed on this section of the route, along the A66 dual carriageway, but it is downhill and half of the distance is on a slip road. After a climb to Barningham the route heads north to Whorlton and then back to Barnard Castle and the Bowes Museum – even if you do not visit the museum itself, cycle into the grounds which are well worth a visit.

Places of interest along the route

A Barnard Castle

Barnard Castle is an attractive market town, with many fine 17th-, 18th- and 19th-century buildings. There has been a settlement here since at least Roman times, and the street Galgate stands on the line of a Roman road which crossed the River Tees by a ford upstream from the castle. The 12th-century **castle** was built by Bernard Baliol and Bernard's castle gave its name to the town that grew up around it. Dominated by an impressive round tower, the remains of the castle are extensive and impressive, and it is easy to see how this was one of northern England's largest Medieval castles. The castle was built on a steep bank of the River Tees and there are riverside walks through the woods that once formed part of the castle's hunting grounds. English Heritage site. Audio tour and gift shop. Picnics welcome. Open April to October, daily 1000–1800 (or dusk if earlier); November to March, Wednesday–Sunday 1000–1300 and 1400–1600. Charge. Telephone 0191-212 3000 for further information. The **Bowes Museum** was the creation of Josephine and John Bowes, between 1862 and 1875. Housed in a chateau, set in a 8ha (20 acre) landscaped park, the museum has a varied and magnificent collection of European paintings, furniture, decorative arts, textiles, costume, archaeology and local history. Open all year, Monday–Saturday 1000–1730, Sunday 1400–1700; March, April and October closes 1700; November to February closes 1600. Charge. Café (free admission) open April to October, museum opening times apply. Telephone (01833) 690606.

The Bowes Museum, Barnard Castle

B Egglestone Abbey, near Barnard Castle
The picturesque site of a ruined 12th-century abbey. Founded in the 1190s by Cistercian monks, the Abbey of St John the Baptist suffered at the hands of both the Scottish and English armies. Adjacent to the abbey is a beautiful example of a Medieval pack horse bridge. English Heritage site. Open at all reasonable times. Admission free. Telephone 0191-212 3000 for further information.

C Whorlton Lido, near Whorlton
Whorlton Lido is a family leisure park situated on the banks of the River Tees with swimming, miniature railway and bus rides, putting green and fishing available. Picnic area and café. Open Easter to September, daily 1000–1900. Charge. Telephone (01833) 627397

Food and drink

There are numerous opportunities for refreshment in Barnard Castle and a café at the Bowes Museum. There are also pubs in Barningham, Smallways, and Hutton Magna, and a shop in Newsham.

Morrit Arms, Greta Bridge
Bar, restaurant and hotel. Bar meals served.

A66 Motel, Smallways
Bar and restaurant. Meals served all day.

The Bridge Inn, Whorlton
Country pub serving real ale and meals.

Route description

Head south from the Tourist Information Centre, to pass the Methodist church on the right, and TR at the TJ (effectively SO), SP Bowes/ Brough. Cycle through the town and SO at roundabout, SP Bowes. Follow road round to right as it becomes Bridgegate, towards the river. At the bottom of the hill cross the bridge and TL at TJ, SP Reeth/Richmond/Scotch Corner. Continue alongside the River Tees.

1 TL along Abbey Lane, SP Egglestone Abbey. Pass the abbey on the right.

2 TR at TJ (effectively SO), SP Greta Bridge/ Richmond.

3 TL at TJ onto the A66. Take great care on this short downhill section.

6km (3.5 miles)

4 TR with care, SP Greta Bridge/Brignall/ Barningham.

5 TL, SP Barningham. Climb into Barningham.

6 TL at TJ, SP Newsham. Cycle downhill to Newsham and through the village.

River Tees

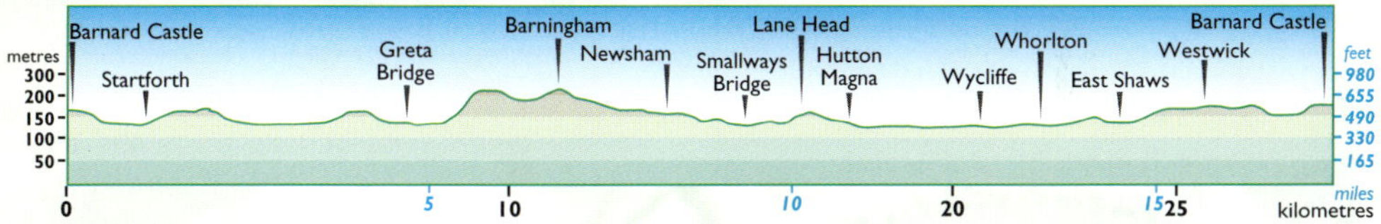

7 SO at XR, SP Hutton Magna/Ovington/Whorlton/Winston. Cross the A66.

8 TL at XR, SP Hutton Magna/Ovington/Winston (16km/10 miles). Enter Hutton Magna.

9 TL, SP Wycliffe/Whorlton. Bear right and pass St Mary's Church on the right.

10 TL at TJ opposite ornamental gates, no SP.

11 TR, SP Whorlton (20.5km/12.5 miles). Descend, pass Whorlton Lido on the right, cross an unusual bridge and climb into Whorlton.

12 TL, SP Barnard Castle. Continue on this flat road all the way to Barnard Castle, passing the Bowes Museum once you are in the town.

13 TR at TJ (roundabout), SP Darlington/Tourist Information and complete the route.

28km (17.5 miles)

Route
10
HAWES AND WIDDALE FELL

Route information

Distance 35.5km (22 miles)

Grade Strenuous

Terrain Tarmac roads throughout, with one hard climb half-way through the route.

Time to allow 2–4 hours.

Getting there by car Hawes is on the A684 Sedbergh road. There are several long term car parks in the town and a pay and display car park at the start of the route – the Dales Countryside Museum/National Park Information Centre. The museum is well signed.

Getting there by train Although there is no railway station at Hawes, the route passes Dent and Garsdale Stations, both on the Settle–Carlisle line. Telephone (0345) 484950 for timetable information.

The route climbs out of Hawes and along Widdale, for a descent into Dentdale, past the spectacular Dent Head Viaduct. A stiff climb along an old coal road (part of the Yorkshire Dales Cycle Way) gives rewarding views of Dentdale and the Artengill Viaduct. A sharp descent to the River Ure takes you back into Hawes.

Places of interest along the route

A Hawes

Market towns are a particular feature of the Yorkshire Dales and Hawes is said to be the highest market town in England. Tuesday is market day and there are several craft workshops. The **Dales Countryside Museum**, housed in the old railway station, explains how the people of the Dales have influenced the evolution of the distinctive Dales landscape. There are exhibits on upland farming, domestic life in the early 20th century, wool and hand-knitting (once a major industry in the area), lead mining, stone cutting, dairying and cheese-making. Hands-on displays and a Time Tunnel, illustrating 10,000 years of Dales history. Gift shop. Open April to October, daily 1000–1700; limited winter opening – telephone for details. Charge. Telephone (01969) 667450. At the **Hawes Ropemakers**, located next to the Countryside Museum, visitors can see traditional ropemaking and learn how the many thin strands of yarn are rapidly twisted into strong rope. The ropeworks manufacture all manner of items, from skipping ropes and dog leads to church bell ropes. Gift shop. Open all year, Monday–Friday 0900–1730; July to October also open Saturday 1000–1730. Free admission. Telephone (01969) 667487. The **Wensleydale Creamery** manufactures real Wensleydale cheese – there is a viewing gallery overlooking the manufacturing area, a museum explaining the history of Wensleydale cheese and a food hall. Guided tours, audio-video presentation, restaurant and coffee shop. The best time to see cheesemaking is between 1030 and 1500. Open all year, Monday–Saturday 0930–1700, Sunday 1000–1630. Charge. Telephone (01969) 667664.

Food and drink

Hawes has plenty of tearooms and numerous pubs, and there are two pubs in Dentdale. Refreshments are also available at the Wensleydale Creamery.

Scow Cottage

Bed and breakfast serving tea and cakes. Delightful setting, with seating inside or out. Open when signposted.

Dent Head Viaduct

Dentdale

Route description

To start the route from Dent Station, leave the station and TR at junction, cross the railway line and continue, passing Garsdale Station on the right; or, TR out of Garsdale Station. In either case continue the route from direction 4.

From the Dales Countryside Museum, TR at TJ, SP Ingleton and follow the one-way system. At the end of the cobbles (also the end of the one-way system) continue SO. Follow the road past the shops to the edge of town.

1 TL onto B6255, SP Ingleton. Pass the youth hostel on the left and gradually climb Widdale.

2 TR, SP Dent/Sedbergh for a descent into Dentdale (10.5km/6.5 miles). Pass Dent Head Viaduct. Continue down, following the River Dee and passing Dent Youth Hostel on the left. Cross the River Dee.

3 TR, SP Dent Station (15.5km/9.5 miles). Climb steeply on switchbacks. Pass Dent Station on the right and cross the railway line. The road flattens for 1.5km (1 mile) then descends, passing Garsdale Station on the right.

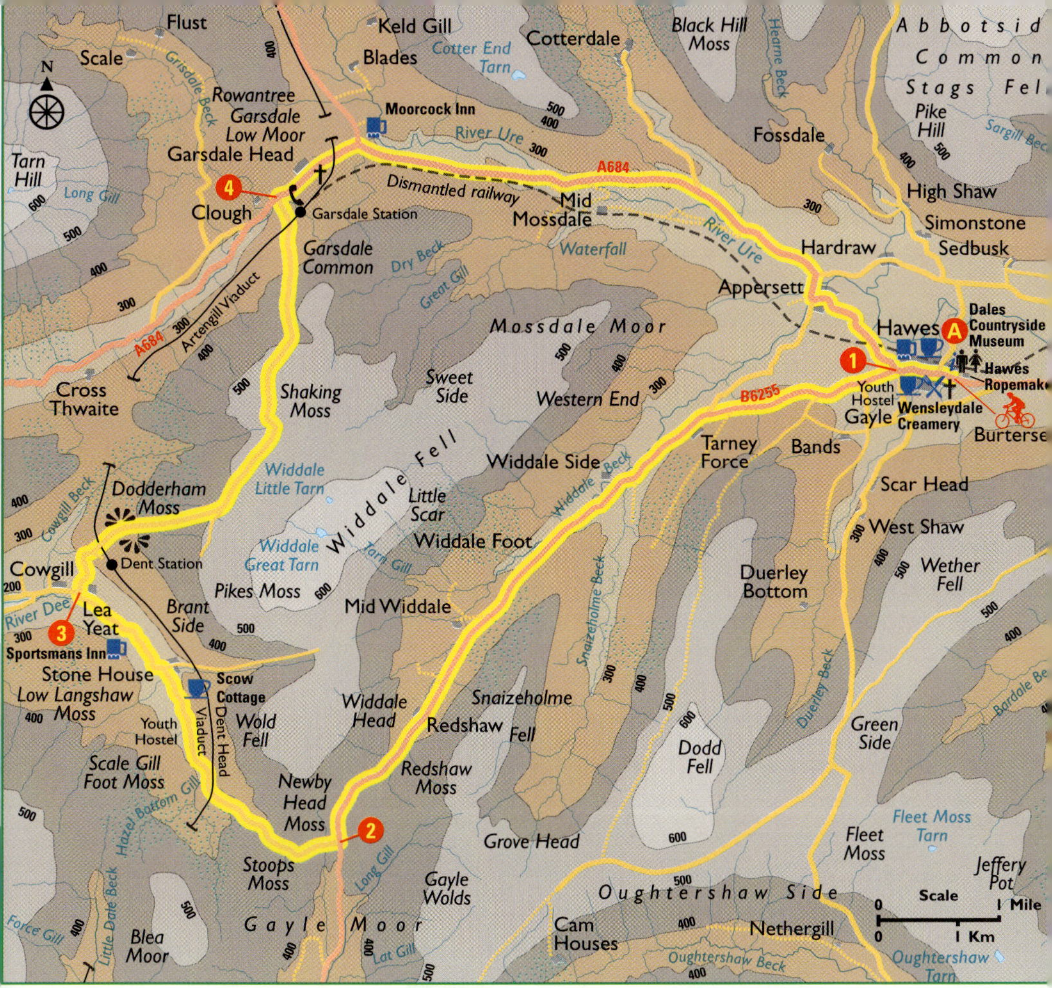

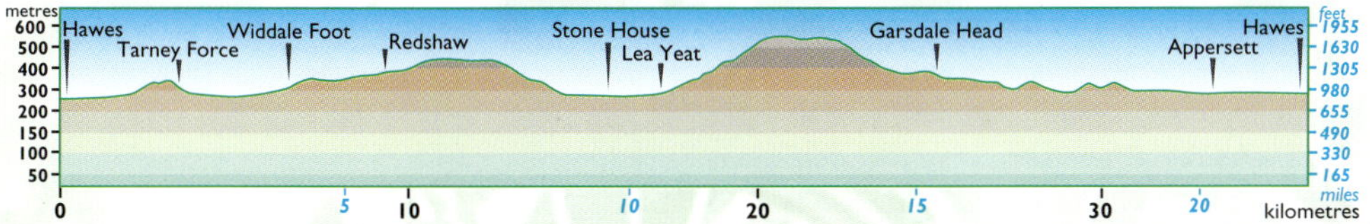

4 TR at TJ onto the A684, SP Hawes (22.5km/14 miles). Pass Hawes Junction Church on the right. Continue under the railway and follow the old railway line and the River Ure through Appersett into Hawes. If you started the route from Dent or Garsdale Stations, continue the route at direction 1 where TR onto B6255. Otherwise, follow the one-way system back to the Dales Countryside Museum.

35.5km (22 miles)

Route 11

SWALEDALE – ASKRIGG TO REETH

Route information

Distance 36km (22.5 miles)

Grade Strenuous

Terrain Two steep climbs and a lovely long downhill section.

Time to allow 2–4 hours.

Getting there by car Askrigg is in Wensleydale in the centre of the Yorkshire Dales. Take the A684 west from Hawes and TL at Bainbridge. Parking is available by the church.

Getting there by train There is no practical rail access to this route.

Starting in Askrigg the route climbs steeply out of Wensleydale – this climb is more than compensated for by the long descent along the southern edge of Swaledale, providing some lovely views. Once through Reeth, a more gentle climb leads back into Wensleydale, via the impressive Bolton Castle. The route passes through Carperby – the village was much used for location shots during the filming of Herriot's All Creatures Great and Small. *A ride along Wensleydale back to Askrigg completes the route.*

Places of interest along the route

A Reeth

The village of Reeth is strategically sited at the junctions of Swaledale and Arkengarthdale, the most northerly of the Yorkshire Dales. There is a large village green, which is still the focal point of many traditional events. Market day is on Friday. The folk museum, craft workshops and tearooms make Reeth a popular place to visit. The **Swaledale Folk Museum** illustrates the local history of the Dales – village life and traditions, religion, farming, mining and knitting and much more. Gift shop. Open Easter to October, daily 1030–1700. Charge. Telephone (01748) 884373. Local crafts have played a large part in the life of the Dales and today's craftworkers continue the tradition of producing high quality goods. Located in the **Dales Centre** in Reeth are the workshops of a cabinet maker (01748) 884555, guitar maker (01748) 884887, clock maker (01748) 884088, artists' studio ((01748) 884663 as well as animal modelling (01748) 884498 and rug making (01748) 884435. Opening times of individual workshops vary, so please telephone to confirm.

B Bolton Castle, near Leyburn

Bolton Castle was built in 1379 for Richard le Scrope, Lord Chancellor of England to Richard II. This is one of the country's best preserved and most impressive castles. Life-size tableaux illustrate the past – the castle chaplain, miller, blacksmith and the bedroom of Mary, Queen of Scots, where she was imprisoned for six months. Also tearoom and gardens. Open March to November, daily 1000–1700. The castle is open December to February but telephone to confirm times. Charge. For further information telephone (01969) 623981.

Swaledale

Food and drink

Askrigg and Reeth both have lots of places for refreshment and there is a tearoom at Bolton Castle.

The Bridge Inn, Grinton
Village pub serving bar meals.

The Wheatsheaf, Carperby
Pub, restaurant and hotel. Bar meals available. James Herriot and his wife Helen spent their honeymoon here in 1941.

Route description

Start in the centre of Askrigg, by St Oswald's Church. Cycle uphill, passing the post office on the right and the King's Arms on the left. Just past the Crown Inn, TL, SP Muker, for the start of a hard climb.

1 TR, SP Reeth, and continue climbing. From the top, continue along this road as it descends along the southern edge of Swaledale.

2 TL, SP Reeth (11km/7 miles). Cross the river and TR at TJ opposite the post box, no SP. Pass through Reeth and Fremington and continue to Grinton.

Askrigg

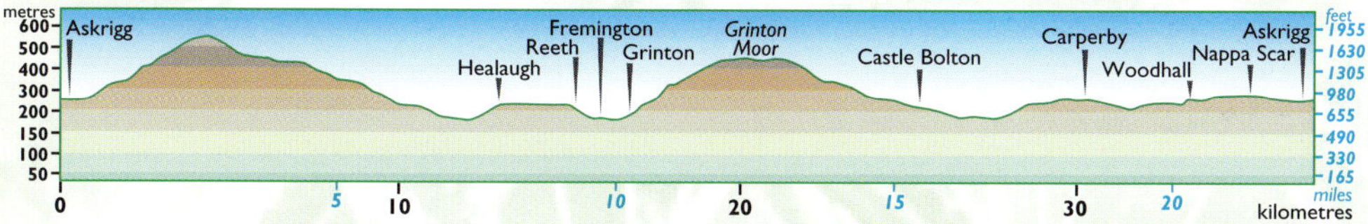

3 Cross the River Swale again and TR, SP Redmire/Leyburn. Climb ahead. ***16km (10 miles)***

4 TR, SP Redmire. Keep climbing, passing the old lead mine workings on either side of the road. Reach the top just after the cattle grid (20.5km/12.5 miles) and descend into Wensleydale. Pass SP 1:7 descent on the left.

5 Soon after SP (1:7), TR, SP Castle Bolton. Cycle along a narrow wooded lane into Castle Bolton. Pass the castle on the right and descend.

6 TR at TJ, SP Carperby/Aysgarth Falls/Askrigg. Cycle along Wensleydale, through Carperby, and return to Askrigg and the end of the route. ***36km (22.5 miles)***

Route **12**

MASHAM AND JERVAULX ABBEY

Route information

Distance 40km (25 miles)

Grade Strenuous

Terrain Mostly quiet, undulating lanes. One off-road section along a firm farm track, which could be tackled by a touring bicycle, although an on-road alternative is offered.

Time to allow 2–5 hours.

Getting there by car Masham is on the eastern side of the Yorkshire Dales, on the A6108, Ripon to Leyburn road. Car parking is available in the large market place except on market days (Wednesday and Saturday).

Getting there by train There is no practical rail access to this ride.

Starting in Masham, this route first heads south on a steady climb with great views. Then, on through Grewelthorpe and close to the edge of the Dales along a firm bridlepath, now heading north. The route climbs further, with a lovely 360 degree view of the Dales. An optional visit to a unique druid temple is worth the uphill effort. The route continues north, via Fearby and Ellingstring, to the remains of a Cistercian abbey. A flat section and a descent take you back into Masham.

Places of interest along the route

A Black Sheep Brewery, Masham

Newly established, but located on the site of a former brewery, the Black Sheep Brewery looks as if it has been on this site for years. The brewhouse is built in the former kiln of the old maltings, in the traditional way. Visitor centre, brewery tours and video presentation, shop and a bistro, situated on the top floor of the maltings. Visitor centre and shop open all year, daily 1000–1730 (January to March closes at 1630). Guided tours take place all year, daily at 1100, 1230, 1400, 1500 and 1600, but telephone to confirm. Bistro open all year, Monday 1000–1700, Tuesday–Sunday 1000–2300 (January to March, closes at 1630). Admission free with charge for brewery tour. Telephone (01765) 689227 for further information.

B Theakston Brewery, Masham

The Theakston Brewery has been on this site in Masham since 1827 and much of the original equipment is still used in the traditional way. Visitor centre and shop, brewery tours. Visitor centre and shop open March, Wednesday and Saturday 1030–1600; Easter to October, daily (except Tuesday) 1030–1600; November to mid-December, Wednesday, Saturday and Sunday 1030–1300 and 1400–1600. Charge. Telephone (01765) 6890457.

C Druid Temple, near Ilton

Created out of large rocks thousands of years ago, this enclosed structure with a single entrance contains standing stones, arches and at the far end a chamber with rock seats. There are other smaller temples on this fascinating site. The view over Leighton Reservoir is breathtaking. Access at all reasonable times. Free. For further information, telephone the Tourist Information Centre in Pateley Bridge on (01423) 711147.

D Jervaulx Abbey, Jervaulx

The abbey was founded in 1156 by Cistercian Monks who arrived from France after the Norman Conquest. The name Jervaulx comes from the Medieval French translation of valley – vaulx – and the River Ure – Jer. In 1536 the last Abbot, Adam Sedbar, joined the rebellion against Henry VIII and the Dissolution. The Abbot was put to death and the abbey was stripped of valuable items and partly demolished.

Food and drink

There is plenty of choice in Masham and an excellent tearoom at Jervaulx Abbey.

The Crown, Grewelthorpe
Bar and restaurant meals.

Black Swan, Fearby
Village pub serving bar meals. Camping available.

Boot and Shoe, Thirn
Bar meals available.

Druid Temple, near Ilton

The ruins seen today are only a small part of the former extensive complex. Unmown lawns and wild flowers make this a beautiful site. Visitor centre, gift shop and tearoom. Abbey open all year, daily during daylight hours. Visitor centre open March to October, daily 1000–1700; November and December, Tuesday–Sunday 1200–1600. Telephone (01677) 460391.

Route description

Start from the market place in Masham. In the opposite corner to the church is a red telephone box and next to this a SP for Swinton/Grewelthorpe – follow this. The road swings to the left, again SP Swinton/Grewelthorpe. Pass Park Street Methodist Church on the right and climb steadily towards Grewelthorpe. Continue into the village or, if following the on-road option:

a TR, SP Kirkby Malzeard/Ilton. Continue along this road following SP Ilton.

b TR at TJ, no SP and continue route at direction 6.

1 TR opposite the pub, SP Kirkby Malzeard. ***5.5km (3.5 miles)***

2 TR, SP The Hutts/Ilton.

3 TL, SP The Hutts/Bramley, then LHF, SP Bramley. Pass Holmes Farm on the left.

4 At Foulgate Farm bear right through the farmyard, keeping the houses to the right. Cycle along a clearly defined, hedged track. Pass a house on the left and later the entrance to Low Bramley Grange.

5 TR at TJ opposite Cindra How, no SP, for a gentle climb. ***9.5km (6 miles)***

6 TL at TJ, SP Ilton. Enter Ilton and bear right. Descend steeply, cross ford and climb.

7 To visit the druid temple,TL, no SP, and climb (14km/8.5 miles). After your visit, retrace route downhill and TL at TJ, no SP, continuing downhill. Otherwise, continue descent SO.

8 TL at bottom of hill, SP Healey. Cross bridge and climb.

9 TR at TJ, SP Fearby/Masham. Cycle through Fearby.

10 TL opposite Kings Head pub, SP Ellington/Ellingstring (20km/12.5 miles). Cycle through ford and continue.

11 TL at TJ, no SP (junction is a small grass triangle). Pass Haregill Lodge on the right.

12 TR, SP Ellingstring, and cycle through this pretty village.

13 TR at TJ, no SP. Follow road as it swings to right, for a fast descent. ***25km (15.5 miles)***

14 To visit Jervaulx Abbey, TL at TJ, SP Middleham/Leyburn/Jervaulx Abbey. Otherwise TR at TJ, SP Masham.

15 TL, SP Bedale. Cross a bridge. The terrain is pretty flat now.

16 TR at XR, no SP (31.5km/19.5 miles). Pass SP Richmondshire on right. Enter Thirn.

17 TR at XR, SP Masham. ***35km (21.5 miles)***

18 TR at TJ, SP Masham (39.5km/24.5 miles). Cross bridge, enter Masham and bear left up hill back to the market place to complete the route. ***40km (25 miles)***

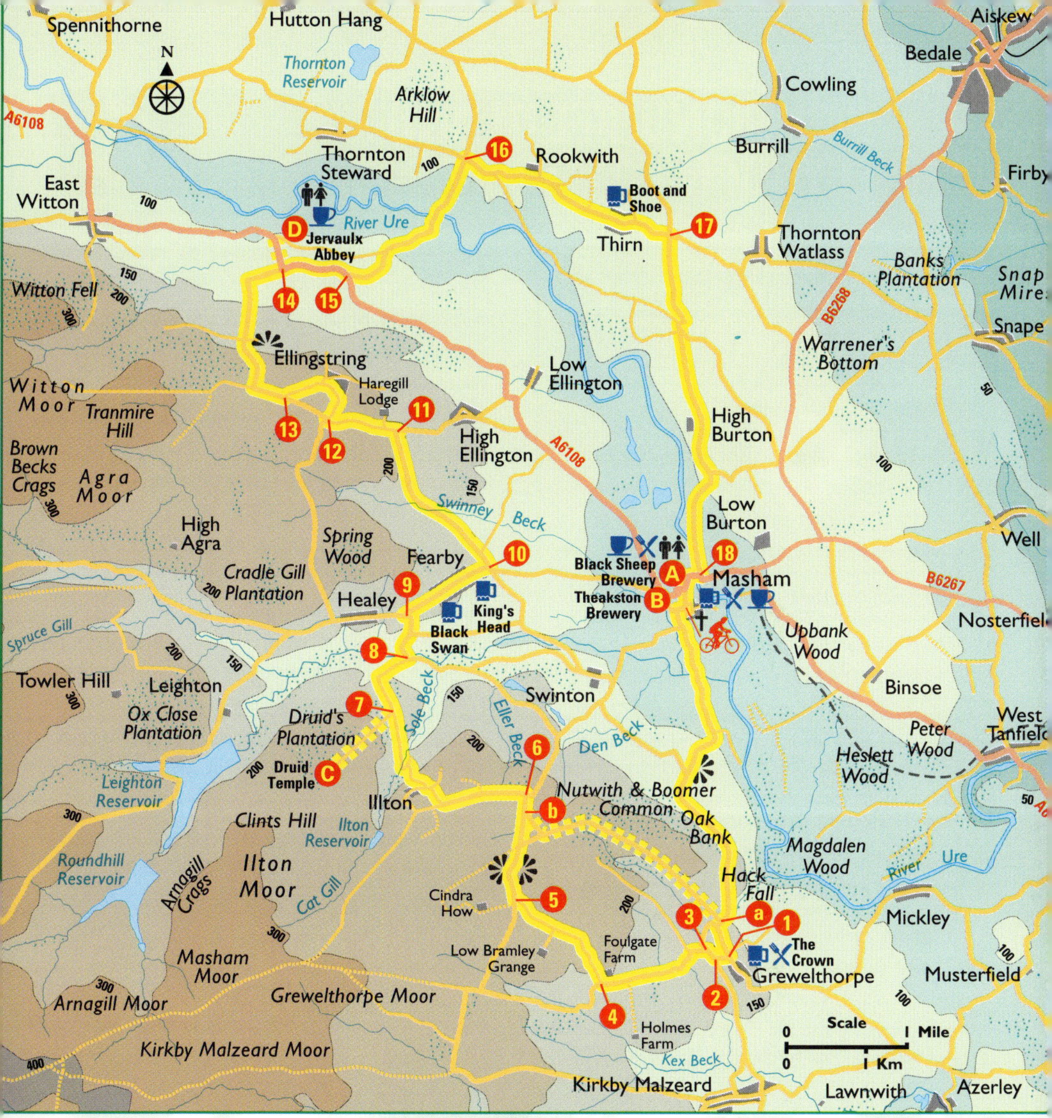

Spennithorne
Hutton Hang
Aiskew
Bedale
Thornton Reservoir
Arklow Hill
Cowling
A6108
Thornton Steward
Rookwith
Burrill
Burrill Beck
Firby
East Witton
Boot and Shoe
River Ure
Jervaulx Abbey
Thirn
Thornton Watlass
Banks Plantation
Snap Mire
Witton Fell
B6268
Snape
Warrener's Bottom
Ellingstring
Haregill Lodge
Low Ellington
Witton Moor
Tranmire Hill
High Ellington
High Burton
Brown Becks Crags
Agra Moor
A6108
Swinney Beck
Low Burton
High Agra
Spring Wood
Fearby
Well
Cradle Gill Plantation
Black Sheep Brewery
Masham
Healey
King's Head
Theakston Brewery
B6267
Black Swan
Upbank Wood
Nosterfield
Spruce Gill
Towler Hill
Leighton
Swinton
Binsoe
Ox Close Plantation
Druid's Plantation
Sole Beck
Ellar Beck
Den Beck
Peter Wood
West Tanfield
Heslett Wood
Druid Temple
Leighton Reservoir
Illton
Nutwith & Boomer Common
Oak Bank
Clints Hill
Illton Reservoir
Magdalen Wood
Roundhill Reservoir
Illton Moor
River Ure
Arnagill Crags
Cat Gill
Hack Fall
Cindra How
Mickley
Masham Moor
Low Bramley Grange
Foulgate Farm
The Crown
Grewelthorpe
Musterfield
Arnagill Moor
Grewelthorpe Moor
Scale
Mile
Km
Holmes Farm
Kirkby Malzeard Moor
Kex Beck
Kirkby Malzeard
Lawnwith
Azerley

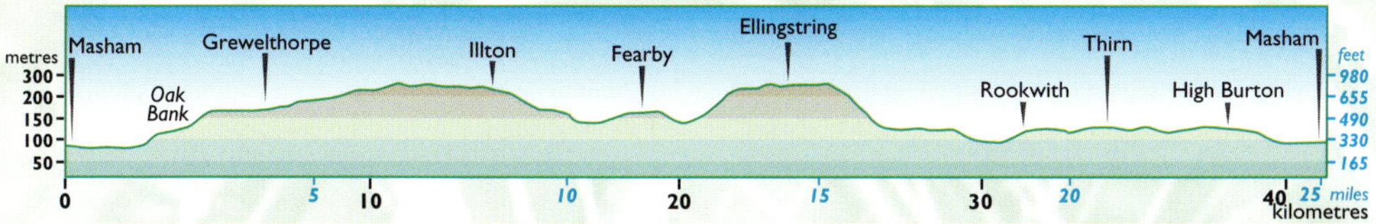

metres
Masham
Oak Bank
Grewelthorpe
Illton
Fearby
Ellingstring
Rookwith
Thirn
High Burton
Masham
feet
300 200 150 100 50
980 655 490 330 165
0 10 20 30 40 kilometres
5 10 15 20 25 miles

Route 13

RICHMOND, REETH AND LEYBURN

Route information

Distance 42km (26 miles)

Grade Strenuous

Terrain A route of climbs and descents, all on minor roads except for a short stretch of A road out of Leyburn.

Time to allow 3–5 hours.

Getting there by car Richmond is to the north east of the Yorkshire Dales on the A6136 and A6108, close to the A1. Long term car parking is available in the town.

Getting there by train There is no practical rail access to this ride.

A triangular route, starting from Richmond for a climb and descent towards Marske and on to Reeth. On from Reeth to Leyburn – one of the easiest crossings in the Dales, but still involving a long steady climb. The final section of the triangle involves a further climb over Hipswell Moor, before returning to Richmond.

Places of interest along the route

A Richmond

Richmond is an attractive town, with cobbled streets and many fine Georgian buildings. The town grew up around **Richmond Castle**. The construction of the castle was begun in 1071 by Alan Rufus, a kinsman of William the Conqueror. It was one of the first in the country to be built of stone – previously timber and earthworks had been used. The impressive keep was added in the 12th century. Its strong defences were never tested. The Great Hall has been floored, re-roofed and partly glazed, to give an idea of what it would have been like in Medieval times. English Heritage property. Picnics welcome. Open April to October, daily 1000–1800 (or dusk if earlier); November to March, daily 1000–1600. Charge. Telephone (01748) 822493 for information. Richmond has three museums. The **Green Howards Museum**, Trinity Church Square, illustrates 300 years of unbroken history of one of the country's oldest regiments. There are artefacts and photographs, uniforms and medals. Audio guide, video presentation and gift shop. Open February, Monday–Friday 1000–1630; March and November, Monday–Saturday 1000–1630; April to October, Monday–Saturday 0930–1630, Sunday 1400–1630; closed December and January. Charge. Telephone (01748) 822133. The award-winning **Richmondshire Museum**, in Ryders Wynd, presents the history of Richmondshire from prehistoric times to the present day. Exhibitions include transport, local industry, geology, toys and James Herriot's surgery. Open Easter to October, 1100–1700. Charge. Telephone (01748) 825611. The **Georgian Theatre Royal and Museum**, Victoria Road, is a unique example of a Georgian theatre, with the majority of its original features. The theatre was built in 1788 by Samuel Butler, an actor/manager. The museum is adjacent to the theatre and contains a unique collection of playbills and the largest complete set of Georgian scenery. Guided tours of the theatre mid-February to March, November and December, Monday–Saturday 1330 and 1630. Guided tours of the theatre and museum Easter to October, Monday–Saturday 1030–1630, Sunday 1100–1330. Charge. Enquiries telephone (01748) 823710; box office telephone (01748) 823021.

B Reeth

The village of Reeth is strategically sited at the junctions of Swaledale and Arkengarthdale, the most northerly of the Yorkshire Dales. There is a large village green, which is still the focal point of many traditional events. Market day is on Friday. The folk museum, craft workshops and tearooms make Reeth a popular place to visit. The **Swaledale Folk Museum** illustrates the local history of the dales – village life and traditions, religion, farming, mining and knitting, and much more. Gift shop. Open Easter to October, daily 1030–1700. Charge. Telephone (01748) 884373. Local crafts have played a large part in the life of the Dales and today's craft-workers continue the tradition of producing high quality goods. Located in the **Dales Centre** in Reeth are the workshops of a cabinet maker (01748) 884555, guitar maker (01748) 884887, clock maker (01748) 884088, artists' studio ((01748) 884663 as well as animal modelling (01748) 884498 and rug making (01748) 884435. Opening times of individual workshops vary, so please telephone to confirm.

Arkengarthdale

C Leyburn

Leyburn is an attractive old market town, with interesting shops and galleries, an antiques auction house and a market each Friday. It is a popular centre for visitors to Wensleydale. The **Tea Pottery**, a purpose-built pottery studio and showroom, produces nothing else but teapots – each one individually cast, hand-painted and decorated. A walkway through the studio, with informative printed panels, leads the visitor through each stage of manufacture. Gift shop; cups of tea available. Studio and gift shop open all year, Monday–Friday 0900–1700; gift shop also open weekends, 0900–1700. Admission free. Telephone (01969) 623839. Also in Leyburn is the **Violin Workshop**. Violins have been made in the same way for hundreds of years and visitors to the workshop can discover how they are created, with lots on hands-on displays, workshop, viewing gallery and video presentation. Gift shop. Open from Easter to June and September, Sunday–Friday 1000–1700, Saturday 1200–1630; July–August, daily 1200–1630. Note no violin manufacture at weekends. Charge. Telephone (01969) 624416.

Food and drink

There are plenty of places for refreshment in Richmond, Reeth and Leyburn.

The Bridge Inn, Grinton
Village pub serving bar meals.

Cross Keys, Bellerby
Bar meals served.

Route description

Start at the Tourist Information Centre and cycle along Victoria Road, away from the roundabout. Take the first TR, opposite the garage, SP P270 spaces. Start climbing and pass the car park on the left. Leave Richmond. The road flattens and you pass two high aerials on the right, after which the road descends quickly into Marske. Continue through the village and cross the bridge.

1 TR at TJ, SP Reeth (9km/5.5 miles). Climb again and then descend towards Reeth.

2 To visit Reeth, TR here for 1km (0.6 mile). After your visit, retrace your route and SO on B6270 to continue route at direction 3. Otherwise, TL at TJ onto B6270, SP Leyburn/Richmond. ***15km (9.5 miles)***

3 TR, SP Leyburn/Redmire. Enter Grinton and climb steeply, passing Grinton Lodge youth hostel on the left, after which the climb is steadier. The flag posts are for the army firing range. Continue towards Leyburn.

4 SO at XR, SP Leyburn (24km/15 miles). Enter Leyburn.

5 To visit Leyburn, TR at TJ and take first TL. After your visit, retrace route and SO here onto A6108, continuing to direction 6. Otherwise, TL at TJ onto A6108, SP Bellerby/Catterick Camp. Cycle through Bellerby.

6 TR at TJ, SP Catterick Camp/Reeth/Richmond. ***31.5km (19.5 miles)***

7 TR (effectively SO), no SP. Climb and then cycle along a straight road littered with tank

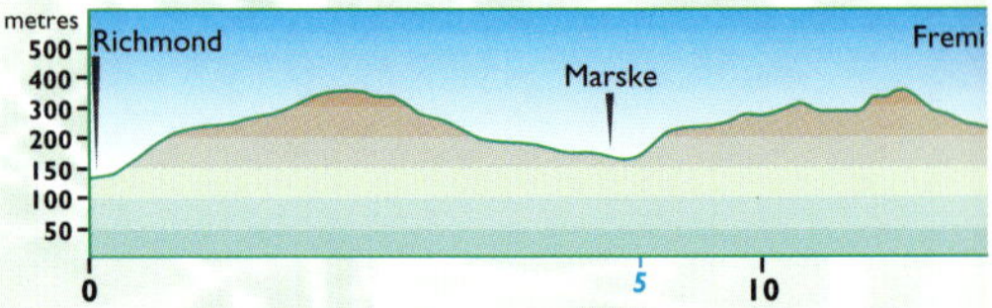

warning signs. Follow this road as it descends and becomes hedged. A steep descent leads to a left hand bend and a further descent produces a good view of Richmond Castle. Cross the bridge.

8 TR into Newbiggin, a cobbled road. Continue as the road bears left and then TR at TJ to return to the Tourist Information Centre and complete the route.

42km (26 miles)

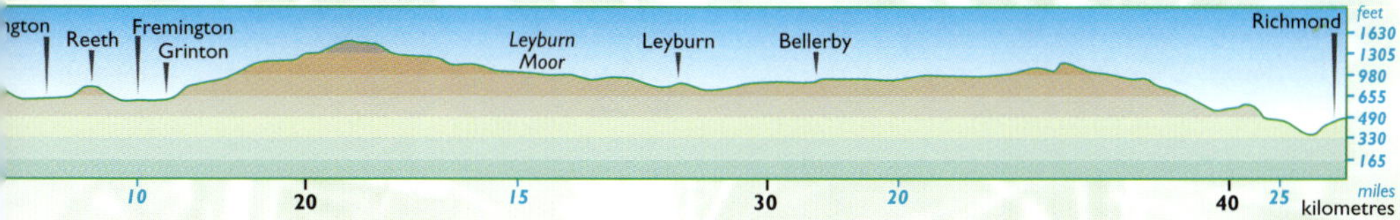

Route 14

MALHAM AND LITTONDALE

Route information

Distance 42.5km (26.5 miles)

Grade Strenuous

Terrain Two long, steep climbs and several steep descents. There is a 3km (2 mile) section of firm off-road around Malham Tarn which is smooth enough for the majority of bicycles – this track has a hard core base and is easily negotiated by all except the most delicate of bicycle rims.

Time to allow 3–5 hours.

Getting there by car Malham is in the southern Dales. Take the minor road north from Gargrave (on the A65 Settle to Skipton road). A pay and display car park is at the southern end of the village, beside the National Park Centre.

Getting there by train The nearest railway station is at Gargrave, 11km (7 miles) from Malham.

A route full of good cycling and fantastic views. Starting from Malham a very steep climb, more than compensated for by lovely views of Malham Cove, takes you towards Malham Tarn. Then, along Silverdale for a good descent into Halton Gill. Scenic Littondale leads you to Arncliffe, whereupon a second steep climb takes you to a solid bridleway leading around the north edge of Malham Tarn. A final grand descent, with extensive southerly views, takes you back into Malham.

Places of interest along the route

A Malham

The village of Malham stands in some of the most magnificent and rugged scenery in the Yorkshire Dales. It is surrounded by some of the best-known glacial landscapes in the country. **Malham Cove** is a limestone cliff of spectacular rock formations, some 85m (280 feet) high. The stream that trickles from the foot of the cove is said to have inspired Charles Kingsley to write the *Water Babies*. **Malham Tarn** is one of the few natural lakes in Yorkshire and incongruous in this usually dry limestone landscape. The naturally formed limestone pavement is home to many different animals and wild flowers and this area is now protected by an agreement between farmers, landowners, the Yorkshire Dales National Park, the Countryside Commission and English Nature. There are newly developed footpaths and bridleways, and existing rights of way where the public can wander at will. The **National Park Centre** in Malham has an exhibition and further information on Malham Cove and Tarn, their history and wildlife. The centre is open April to October, daily 0930–1700. Free. Telephone (01729) 830363.

Rock formation, Malham Cove

Route description

If starting from Gargrave Station, cycle through Gargrave and take the minor road north, following SP Malham. Take care as this scenic road can get busy in the summer. You will pass the National Park Centre on your way into Malham.

Otherwise, if starting from Malham, TL out of the National Park Centre, no SP. Continue SO through the village centre and tackle the very hard climb (1:6 gradient). Views of Malham Cove on the right. Cross cattle grid. The road descends gently.

1 TL at XR, SP Langcliffe/Settle. Malham Tarn is in the distance on the right.

2 Cross cattle grid and TL at TJ, SP Langcliffe/Settle (6km/3.5 miles). Climb to a summit of 435m (1427 feet), then descend. A beautiful view opens up to the left.

3 TR, SP Stainforth, and descend. Take care on this 1:5 descent – it could be slippery. Follow the road as it climbs again (1:6 gradient).

4 TR at TJ, SP Halton Gill, and climb (10.5km/6.5 miles). You are now in Silverdale. Continue towards Halton Gill – along a stone-walled road, across a cattle grid, to the top of the hill (14.5km/9 miles) and descend.

5 TR, SP Litton/Arncliffe (21km/13 miles). Continue descent through Litton to Arncliffe. Follow road as it bears right, SP Kilnsey/Grassington (28km/17.5 miles). Enter Arncliffe, cross bridge and bear left, passing church on left.

6 TR, SP Malham. Cycle through Arncliffe, cross bridge and bear left, SP Malham. Continue along stone-walled road and climb steeply. Cross cattle grid (29.5km/18.5 miles) onto open moorland and single track road with passing places. Take care as you descend the steep, switchbacked road. Climb again, cross four cattle grids, reach the top (35.5km/22 miles) and descend.

7 Just before gate TL, SP Malham Field Centre. Pass postbox in wall on right. Follow track around back of Field Study Centre, through the car park and down the track. Pass through a gate to reveal great views across the Tarn. Continue along the track.

8 SO at XR, SP Malham (39km/24 miles). The road is flat and then descends steeply, with great views south.

9 TR at TJ, SP Village Centre.

10 TL at TJ, SP Hellifield/Settle/Skipton.

11 TR to National Park Centre and the end of the route. ***42.5km (26.5 miles)***

Food and drink

There are several teashops and pubs in Malham and a pub in Arncliffe.

Queen's Arms, Litton

Bed and breakfast, bar meals and beer garden.

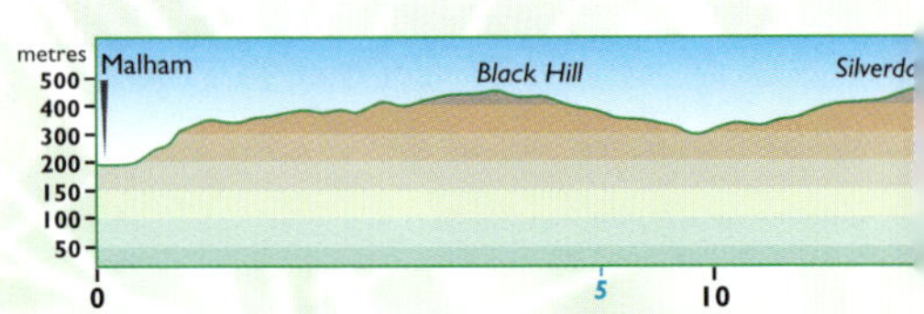

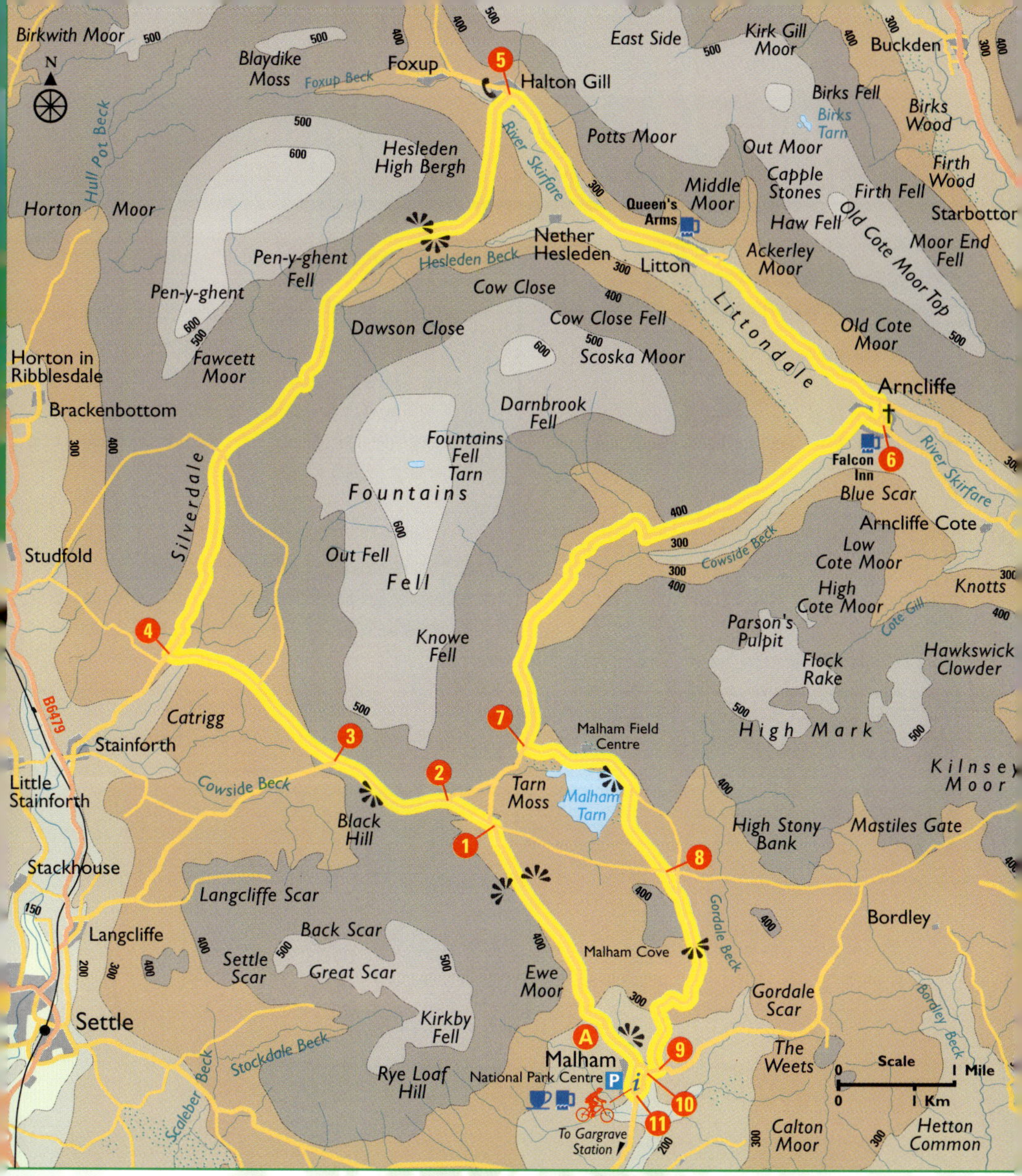
Birkwith Moor
Blaydike Moss
Foxup Beck
Foxup
Halton Gill
East Side
Kirk Gill Moor
Buckden
Birks Fell
Birks Tarn
Birks Wood
Hull Pot Beck
Hesleden High Bergh
River Skirfare
Potts Moor
Out Moor
Capple Stones
Middle Moor
Queen's Arms
Firth Fell
Firth Wood
Starbotton
Horton Moor
Haw Fell
Old Cote Moor Top
Moor End Fell
Pen-y-ghent Fell
Hesleden Beck
Nether Hesleden
Litton
Ackerley Moor
Pen-y-ghent
Cow Close
Cow Close Fell
Littondale
Old Cote Moor
Dawson Close
Scoska Moor
Horton in Ribblesdale
Fawcett Moor
Arncliffe
Brackenbottom
Darnbrook Fell
Fountains Fell Tarn
Falcon Inn
River Skirfare
Fountains
Blue Scar
Silverdale
Arncliffe Cote
Cowside Beck
Low Cote Moor
Studfold
Out Fell
Fell
High Cote Moor
Knotts
Parson's Pulpit
Cote Gill
Knowe Fell
Flock Rake
Hawkswick Clowder
B6479
Catrigg
Malham Field Centre
High Mark
Stainforth
Kilnsey Moor
Little Stainforth
Cowside Beck
Tarn Moss
Malham Tarn
Black Hill
High Stony Bank
Mastiles Gate
Stackhouse
Langcliffe Scar
Bordley
Langcliffe
Back Scar
Gordale Beck
Settle Scar
Great Scar
Malham Cove
Ewe Moor
Gordale Scar
Settle
Kirkby Fell
The Weets
Bordley Beck
Stockdale Beck
Malham
Rye Loaf Hill
National Park Centre
Scale
Mile
Km
Scaleber Beck
To Gargrave Station
Calton Moor
Hetton Common
N
1
2
3
4
5
6
7
8
9
10
11
A

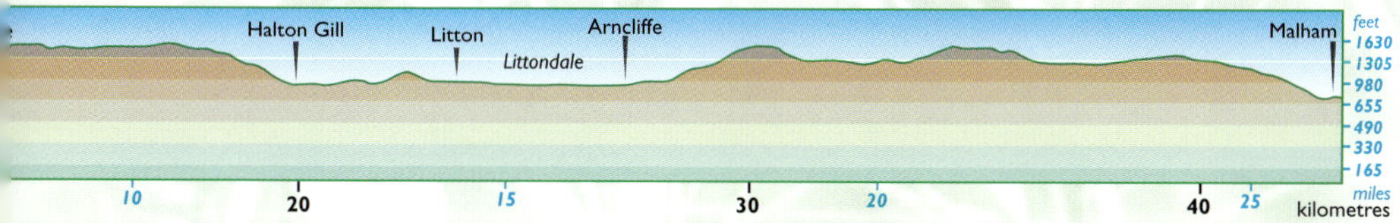
Halton Gill
Litton
Littondale
Arncliffe
Malham
feet
1630
1305
980
655
490
330
165
10
20
15
30
20
40
25
miles
kilometres

Route 15

KINGSDALE – INGLETON TO DENT

Route information

Distance 47.5km (29.5 miles)

Grade Strenuous

Terrain Two steep climbs, in to and out of Dentdale.

Time to allow 3–5 hours.

Getting there by car Ingleton is in the southern Dales, on the A65 Skipton to Kirkby Lonsdale road.

Getting there by train There is no railway station at Ingleton but cyclists could join this route from Dent Station, on the Settle–Carlisle line. Telephone (0345) 484950 for timetable information.

From Ingleton, the route heads towards Thornton in Lonsdale before climbing up Kingsdale and into Dentdale, cycling through the attractive village of Dent. From here, the route heads up past Dent Head Viaduct and the magnificent 24-arch Ribblehead Viaduct. A descent along a gated road takes you back to Ingleton.

Places of interest along the route

A Ingleton

Ingleton's waterfalls are set in ancient oak woodland where two rivers, the Doe and the Twiss, cascade down limestone gorges. There has been a formal walk here since 1885. Well-maintained paths take the visitor upstream

along the Twiss and then back down alongside the Doe, a walk of 7km (4.5 miles). Refreshments available. Open all year, daily 0900–dusk. Nominal charge. Telephone (015242) 41930 for further information. There are many caves and pot holes in the limestone around Ingleton. **White Scar Caves** are open to the public. See route 16 for information.

B Dent

A charming village located in the secluded valley of Dentdale and watched over by Whernside, the highest peak in the Yorkshire Dales National Park at 736m (2414 feet). The main street retains its original cobbles and colour-washed stone cottages. Dent was the birthplace of Adam Sedgwick, a great Victorian geologist, and there is a memorial to him in the centre of the village. The village was once famous for its thriving hand knitting industry and now has some interesting workshops and galleries. Tourist information is available from the Stone Close Restaurant in Dent, or from the Tourist Information Centre in Ingleton, telephone (015242) 41049.

C Dent Head and Ribblehead Viaducts

These viaducts are part of England's most scenic mainline railway, the Settle–Carlisle line. The railway comprises 20 major viaducts and 14 tunnels and was built between 1869 and 1875, with huge loss of life among the navvies constructing the line across the fells and bogs of the Yorkshire Dales. Dent Station (6.5km/ 4 miles) from Dent village, is the highest main line station in England. The Dent Head viaduct, spanning Dentdale, has 10 arches. Ribblehead Viaduct is the best known and probably most photographed viaduct on the Settle–Carlisle line. Its 24 arches span Batty Moss below, the site of a former navvy encampment. For further information, telephone the Settle–Carlisle information line on (0660) 660607 or National Rail Enquiries on (0345) 484950.

Ribblehead Viaduct

Route description

If starting from Dent Station, leave the station and TL at TJ. Cycle into Lea Yeat where TL, SP Ingleton/Dent Youth Hostel and continue, passing Dent Head Viaduct, to direction 7.

Otherwise, leave Ingleton Tourist Information Centre and TR at TJ, SP Kendal/Skipton/Village Centre. Continue to XR where TR, SP Village Centre. Then TR at TJ onto Main Street, SP Village Centre.

1 TL, SP Thornton in Lonsdale, then TL at TJ, no SP, and cross bridge. Pass the entrance to Ingleton's Waterfalls on the right.

2 TR, SP Thornton in Lonsdale/Dent.

3 TR, SP Dent (telephone and seat on left just after junction). Continue along this road, with its climbs and descents, for 15km (9.5 miles) towards Dent.

4 TL at TJ, SP Dent/Sedbergh (17.5km/ 11 miles), and cycle into Dent.

5 Sharp TR by the George and Dragon pub, SP Hawes/Ingleton (via Newby Head). Continue out of village, crossing bridge, on flat, well-surfaced road. Cycle through Cowgill, passing church on left.

6 If you started the route from Dent Station, TL here and return to the station. Otherwise, follow road to right, SP Ingleton/Dent Youth Hostel (25km/15.5 miles). Pass the Sportsman's Inn on the right (26km/16 miles), cross a bridge, pass Scow Cottage on the left and climb past Dent Head Viaduct (29km/18 miles). Remember to look back at the view.

7 TR at TJ onto B6255, SP Ingleton/ Settle (30.5km/19 miles). Continue along this road, passing Ribblehead Viaduct. Continue past Old Hill Inn. ***37km (23 miles)***

8 TR, SP Chapel-le-Dale Church (40km/ 25 miles). Continue along this narrow, gated road. Pass a second entrance to Ingleton Waterfalls (45km/28 miles). Descend into Ingleton.

9 TL at TJ, no SP. Then, TL along one-way system, following the road as it bends left. TR at TJ, SP Village Centre.

10 If you started the route from Dent Station, follow SP for Village Centre and continue route from direction 1. Otherwise, TR for Tourist Information Centre and the end of the route. ***47.5km (29.5 miles)***

Food and drink

There are numerous opportunities for refreshment in Ingleton and at the waterfalls car park. Dent has two pubs, several tearooms, a restaurant and a convenience store.

Morton Arms Hotel, Thornton-in-Lonsdale
Tea, coffee and meals available.

Scow Cottage
Bed and breakfast with tearoom.

Caravan, Ribble Head
Caravan serving tea, coffee and snacks, with a marvellous view of the Ribble-head Viaduct.

The Station Inn, Ribble Head
Bed and breakfast, real ale and garden. Meals served daily.

Old Hill Inn, Weathercote
Towards the end of the route. Bar meals served.

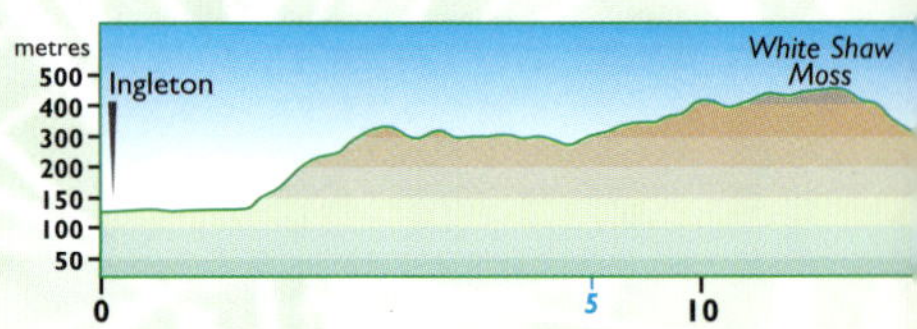

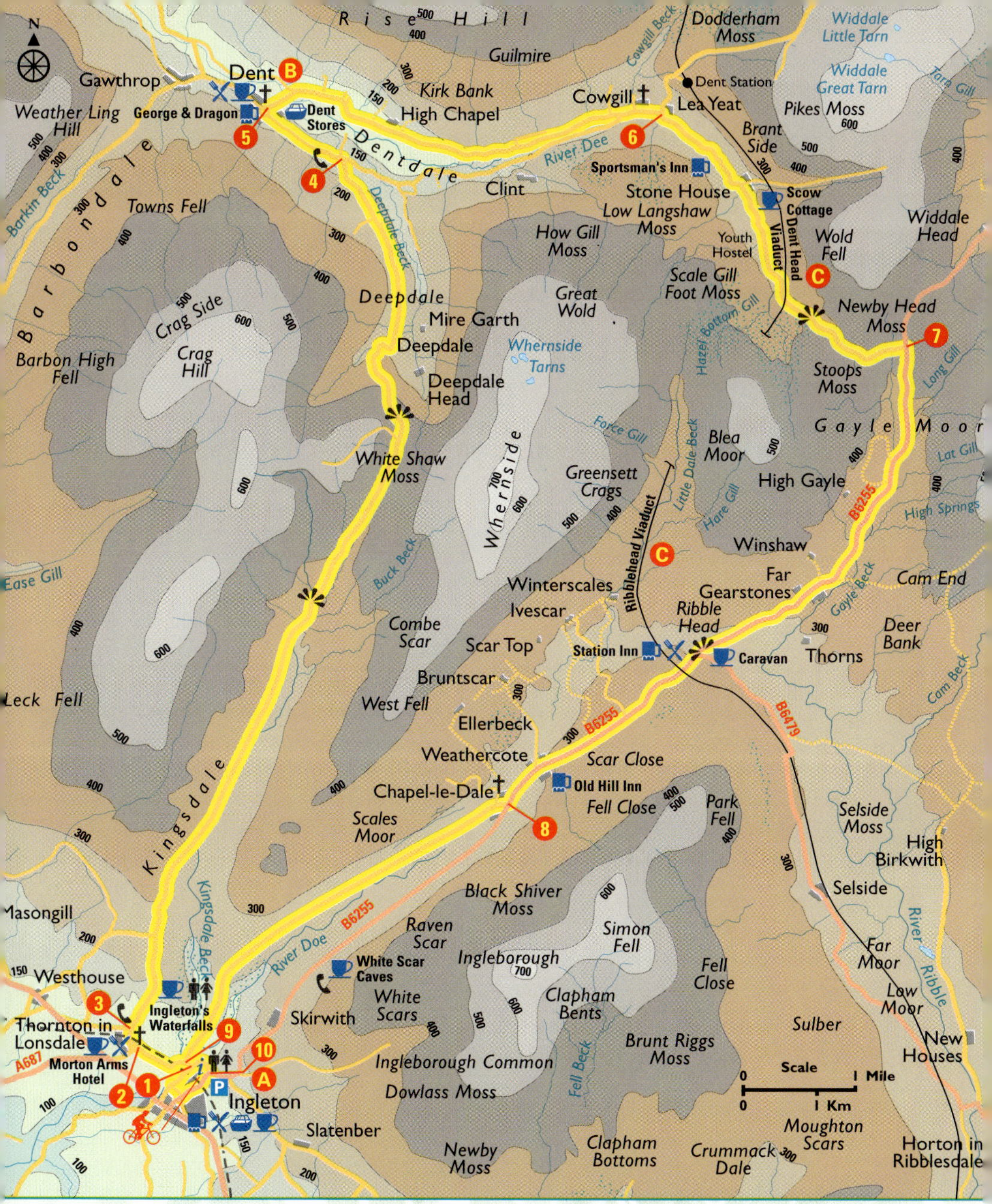
Rise Hill
Dent
Gawthrop
George & Dragon
Dent Stores
Dentdale
Kirk Bank
High Chapel
Cowgill
Lea Yeat
Dent Station
Dodderham Moss
Widdale Little Tarn
Widdale Great Tarn
Pikes Moss
Brant Side
Sportsman's Inn
Stone House
Low Langshaw Moss
Scow Cottage
Dent Head Viaduct
Youth Hostel
Wold Fell
Widdale Head
Newby Head Moss
Stoops Moss
Gayle Moor
Blea Moor
High Gayle
Winshaw
Far Gearstones
Ribble Head
Caravan
Thorns
Cam End
Deer Bank
Station Inn
Ribblehead Viaduct
Winterscales
Ivescar
Scar Top
Bruntscar
Ellerbeck
Weathercote
Chapel-le-Dale
Scar Close
Old Hill Inn
Fell Close
Park Fell
Deepdale
Mire Garth
Deepdale Head
Whernside Tarns
Whernside
Greensett Crags
White Shaw Moss
Great Wold
How Gill Moss
Clint
Towns Fell
Barbondale
Barbon High Fell
Crag Side
Crag Hill
Weather Ling Hill
Leck Fell
Kingsdale
Combe Scar
West Fell
Scales Moor
Masongill
Westhouse
Thornton in Lonsdale
Morton Arms Hotel
Ingleton's Waterfalls
Ingleton
Skirwith
Slatenber
White Scar Caves
White Scars
Raven Scar
Black Shiver Moss
Ingleborough
Simon Fell
Clapham Bents
Ingleborough Common
Dowlass Moss
Newby Moss
Clapham Bottoms
Crummack Dale
Brunt Riggs Moss
Fell Close
Sulber
Moughton Scars
Selside Moss
High Birkwith
Selside
Far Moor
Low Moor
New Houses
Horton in Ribblesdale
B6255
B6479
A687
Scale
0 1 Mile
0 1 Km

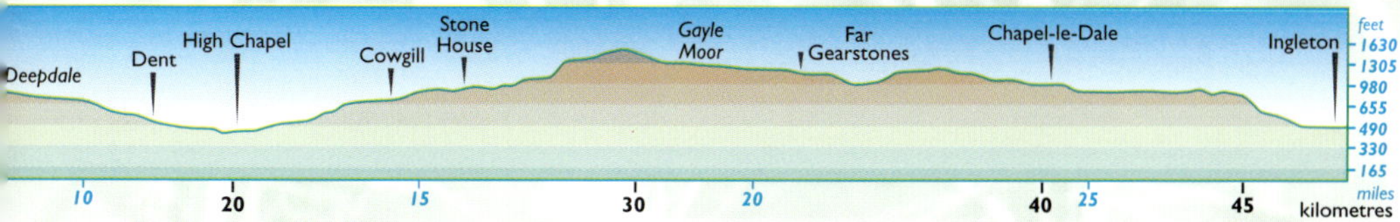
Deepdale
Dent
High Chapel
Cowgill
Stone House
Gayle Moor
Far Gearstones
Chapel-le-Dale
Ingleton
feet
1630
1305
980
655
490
330
165
10
20
15
30
20
40
25
45
miles
kilometres

Route **16**

SETTLE, RIBBLE HEAD AND INGLETON

Route information

Distance 48km (30 miles)

Grade Moderate

Terrain Half of the ride is over B roads, and the rest of the route is on a mix of quiet minor roads and good quality bridleways.

Time to allow 3–6 hours.

Getting there by car Settle is on the south western edge of the Yorkshire Dales National Park, just north of the A65. There is a long stay car park in the town.

Getting there by train Settle is on the Carlisle–Settle line. Telephone (0345) 484950 for information.

A steady climb out of Settle leads to the B6479, as it winds its way up Ribblesdale. Through Horton in Ribblesdale and on to the attractive Ribblehead Viaduct. A short climb and then a lovely stretch of downhill to Ingleton, passing stunning Dales scenery. Then on to Ingleborough and Clapham, from where a series of well-surfaced bridleways take you to on a fast descent back to Settle.

Places of interest along the route

A Settle

The southern Dales are a mix of remote fells and gritstone moors, limestone cliffs and gorges, and lush pastures and valleys. Settle, one of the Dales' many attractive market towns, sits amongst this splendour, beside the largest outcrop of limestone in Britain, an area of caves, cliffs and potholes. It is also on the Carlisle–Settle railway – the country's most arduous railway line with a gradient of 1 in 100. The line was constructed between 1869 and 1876 and still runs a regular passenger service, with occasional special services of steam trains. Market day is Tuesday, and the market square is flanked by interesting 17th- and 18th-century buildings and the Shambles, where the butchers were originally sited. The **Watershed Mill Visitor Centre** is housed in an 1820s cotton mill, beside the River Ribble. The centre is an outlet for Dales-made local crafts – woodwork, pottery, leatherwork, paintings, prints and textiles. Craft demonstrations are held regularly. There is also a rock and fossil shop and a coffee shop. Open all year, Monday–Saturday 1000–1730, Sunday 1100–1730. Admission free. Telephone (01729) 825539 for information.

B Ribblehead Viaduct

Ribblehead Viaduct is one of the Settle–Carlisle line's 20 major viaducts. It is one of the best known and probably the most photographed, with its 24 arches spanning Batty Moss below, the site of a former navvy encampment. For further information, telephone the Settle–Carlisle information line on (0660) 660607 or National Rail Enquiries on (0345) 484950.

C White Scar Caves, Ingleton

There are many caves and pot holes in the limestone scenery around Ingleton. White Scar Caves are 2.5km (1.5 miles) outside Ingleton and were discovered in 1923. The whole system of caves is lit by electricity and the features are floodlit. The 1.5km (1 mile) guided tour takes approximately 80 minutes. Tearoom. Open daily, weather permitting, from 0900 with last tour at 1730. Charge. For further information, contact Ingleton Tourist Information Centre on (015242) 41049. **Ingleton's Waterfalls** are set in ancient woodland where two rivers, the Doe and the Twiss, cascade down limestone gorges. See route 15 for information.

D Ingleborough Cavern, Clapham

Impressive cave formations, underground streams and natural passages. Visitors can see cave coral, illuminated pools and fossils. The cavern is approached along a nature trail through attractive woodland. Guided tours. Picnic area and shop selling soft drinks, snacks and guide books. Open March to October, daily from 1000 with last tour at 1700. Charge. Telephone (015242) 51242.

A typical Dales scene

Route description

TR out of Settle Station, SP Town Centre. TL at TJ (opposite police station) and cycle through town centre. Pass under railway bridge and cross the River Ribble, into Giggleswick.

1 TR, SP Stackhouse/Little Stainforth, climbing steadily up the valley. Reach open moorland and descend.

2 TR at XR opposite quarry (6.5km/4 miles), descend and cross bridge over railway and river.

3 TL at TJ, SP Horton in Ribblesdale/Hawes/B6479(B6255). Continue through Horton in Ribblesdale (10.5km/6.5 miles). Keep on the B6479 through Selside (10km/16 miles) and on to Ribble Head.

4 TL at TJ, SP Ingleton/B6255/White Scar Caves/Station (20.5km/12.5 miles). Views of Ribblehead Viaduct to the right. Stay on this road, all the way down the valley towards Ingleton, passing the entrance to the White Scar Caves (27.5km/17 miles) on the left.

5 TL, SP Clapham (30.5km/19 miles). Continue up this quiet road, passing High Leys Farm. Then down sharp hill (1:7) into Clapham.

6 Arrive Clapham and immediately TL into Eggshell Lane (36km/22.5 miles). Pass SP Unsuitable for Lorries or Coaches and entrance to Ingleborough Cavern on the left. Continue around bend.

7 TL along Church Avenue, no SP. Pass church on left.

8 TL by church, onto byway SP BW Austwick. Pass through tunnel – the first 200m of the track is quite rocky and you may need to walk. However, it soon changes to a good firm surface.

9 SO at XR with tarmac road.

10 TR at TJ opposite iron railings, onto tarmac.

11 Pass SP 30mph and barn on the left. Immediately TL, SP BW Feizor (40km/25 miles). Cross small bridge.

12 SO at XR of byways. The track is smooth, then a little rocky, as it hugs a wall to the left. Cross a small stream via sleepers.

13 Next to broken down barn, take RHF.

14 SO at XR, SP Settle, onto tarmac.

15 TL at TJ, no SP (44km/27.5 miles). The road descends quickly before flattening out in Giggleswick. Continue into Settle and return to the station and the end of the route.

48km (30 miles)

Food and drink

There are lots of places for refreshment in Settle; a shop, tearoom and pubs in Horton in Ribblesdale; and several pubs and cafés in Clapham. There is also a tearoom at White Scar Caves and snacks are available at Ingleborough Cavern.

Helwith Bridge Hotel, Helwith Bridge
Tea, coffee and food served all day.

Golden Lion Hotel, Horton in Ribblesdale
Hotel and pub. Real ale, and bar and restaurant meals.

Pen-y-ghent Café, Horton in Ribblesdale
On the Pennine Way. Nice tearoom selling large mugs of tea, hot chocolate and coffee together with food. Also Tourist Information Centre. Closed Tuesday.

Caravan, Ribble Head
Caravan serving tea, coffee and snacks, with a marvellous view of the Ribblehead Viaduct.

The Station Inn, Ribble Head
Bed and breakfast, real ale and garden. Meals served daily.

Old Hill Inn, Weathercote
Towards the end of the route. Bar meals served.

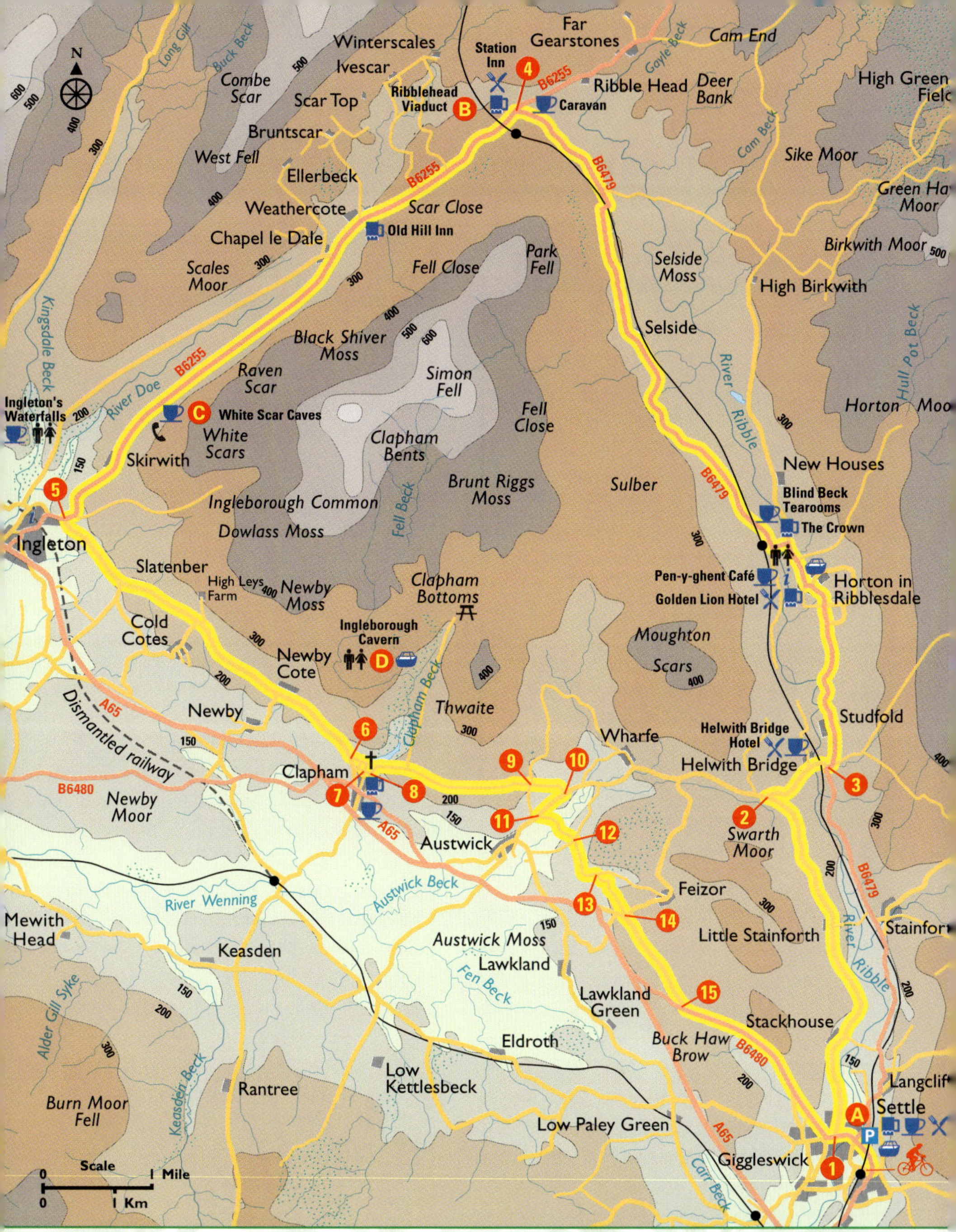
N
Winterscales
Far Gearstones
Cam End
Ivescar
Station Inn
4
B6255
Ribble Head
Deer Bank
Combe Scar
Scar Top
Ribblehead Viaduct
B
Caravan
Bruntscar
West Fell
Ellerbeck
B6479
Sike Moor
Weathercote
Scar Close
Chapel le Dale
Old Hill Inn
Birkwith Moor
Scales Moor
Fell Close
Park Fell
Selside Moss
High Birkwith
Black Shiver Moss
Selside
Simon Fell
Raven Scar
B6255
Ingleton's Waterfalls
River Doe
C
White Scar Caves
Clapham Bents
Fell Close
Horton
White Scars
Skirwith
Brunt Riggs Moss
Sulber
New Houses
5
Ingleborough Common
Blind Beck Tearooms
The Crown
Dowlass Moss
Ingleton
Slatenber
Pen-y-ghent Café
Horton in Ribblesdale
High Leys Farm
Newby Moss
Clapham Bottoms
Golden Lion Hotel
Cold Cotes
Ingleborough Cavern
Moughton Scars
Newby Cote
D
Dismantled railway
Newby
A65
Thwaite
Studfold
Wharfe
Helwith Bridge Hotel
6
Helwith Bridge
9
10
3
Clapham
B6480
7
8
Newby Moor
2
11
Swarth Moor
Austwick
12
Feizor
River Wenning
Austwick Beck
13
14
Mewith Head
Keasden
Austwick Moss
Little Stainforth
Lawkland
Fen Beck
15
Lawkland Green
Stackhouse
Alder Gill Syke
Buck Haw Brow
Eldroth
B6480
Low Kettlesbeck
Rantree
Burn Moor Fell
Keasden Beck
A
Settle
Low Paley Green
A65
Giggleswick
1
Carr Beck
Scale
0
1 Mile
0
1 Km

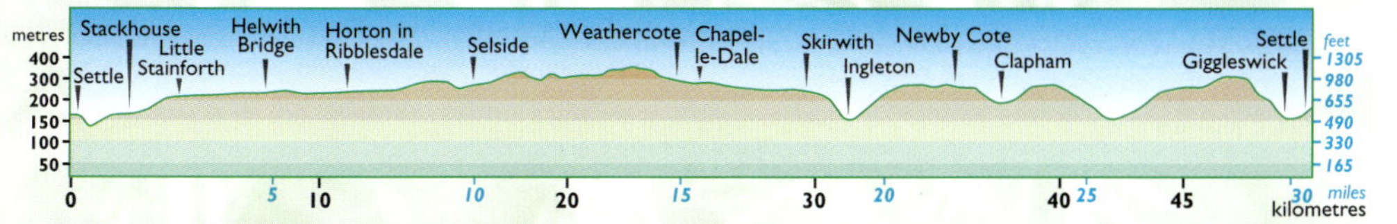
metres
400
300
200
150
100
50
Stackhouse
Settle
Little Stainforth
Helwith Bridge
Horton in Ribblesdale
Selside
Weathercote
Chapel-le-Dale
Skirwith
Ingleton
Newby Cote
Clapham
Giggleswick
Settle
feet
1305
980
655
490
330
165
0
5
10
10
20
15
30
20
40
25
45
30
miles
kilometres

Route 17

COVERDALE, BISHOPDALE AND WHARFEDALE

Route information

Distance 60km (37.5 miles)

Grade Strenuous

Terrain This route takes in three Dales and there is a lot of climbing involved. The first climb out of Kettlewell is the steepest.

Time to allow 4–6 hours.

Getting there by car Kettlewell is near the centre of the Yorkshire Dales, north of Wharfedale. Going north from Skipton, take the B6265 and then the B6160 to Kettlewell. Car parking is available as you enter the village.

Getting there by train There is no practical railway access to this ride.

Starting from Kettlewell with the hardest climb of the route first, taking you into Coverdale. The high moorland descends into walled fields as the route continues through Horsehouse and Carlton to Wensley. Then west to the impressive Bolton Castle and past James Herriot's honeymoon spot for a descent into scenic Aysgarth. A steep climb, followed by a comparatively gentle ride along Bishopdale before the final climb into Wharfedale, leading you back to Kettlewell.

Places of interest along the route

A White Rose Candle Workshop, Wensley

Located in a 19th-century watermill, the workshop manufactures candles of all types and visitors can see the various traditional dipping and casting methods involved. The gift shop stocks a comprehensive range of candles and candle holders. Scenic waterfall. Opening times vary between February and May (telephone for details); June to November, Sunday–Tuesday and Thursday–Friday 1000–1700 (or dusk if earlier); December usually open Sunday 1000–dusk. Telephone (01969) 623544 for further information.

B Bolton Castle, near Leyburn

Bolton Castle was built in 1379 for Richard le Scrope, Lord Chancellor of England to Richard II. This is one of the country's best preserved and most impressive castles. Life-size tableaux illustrate the past – the castle chaplain, miller, blacksmith and the bedroom of Mary, Queen of Scots, where she was imprisoned for six months. Also tearoom and gardens. Open March to November, daily 1000–1700. The castle is open December to February but telephone to confirm times. Charge. For further information telephone (01969) 623981.

C Aysgarth

The River Ure flows through Aysgarth and, beside a 16th-century bridge, flows over a series of flat limestone blocks – **Aysgarth Falls.** The falls will be at their most spectacular after heavy rain, but are magnificent at any time. Admission by honesty box. For more informa-

Aysgarth Falls

tion, telephone the National Park Centre in Aysgarth on (01969) 663424. The **Yorkshire Carriage Museum** is housed in a 200-year-old mill overlooking Aysgarth Falls. There are 57 genuine Victorian carriages on display together with collections of postcards of horsedrawn carriages and hand-made scale models. Open March to October, daily 0930–dusk; November to February, daily 1200–dusk. Telephone (01969) 663399.

Route description

Start on the south side of Kettlewell, beside the telephone box and bridge over the River Wharfe (opposite the Racehorses Hotel and Blue Bell Hotel). Cycle into the village, SP Coverdale. SO at staggered XR, SP Leyburn (gradient 1 in 4). Pass SP Unsuitable for Heavy Vehicles and continue up single track road, that is steep in places.

Food and drink

Kettlewell and Aysgarth have plenty of pubs and tearooms, and refreshments are available at Bolton Castle. There is a shop in Thoralby and a restaurant and tearoom in Buckden. The final stretch of the route is filled with pubs, all indicated on the map.

Post Office, Horsehouse
Also sells tea and coffee.

Thwaite Arms, Horsehouse
Village pub, serving bar meals.

The Foresters Arms, Carlton
Extensive menu, Egon Ronay recommended.

Three Horseshoes, Wensley
Bar snacks available.

Wheatsheaf, Carperby
Pub, restaurant and hotel. Bar meals available. James Herriot and his wife Helen spent their honeymoon here in 1941.

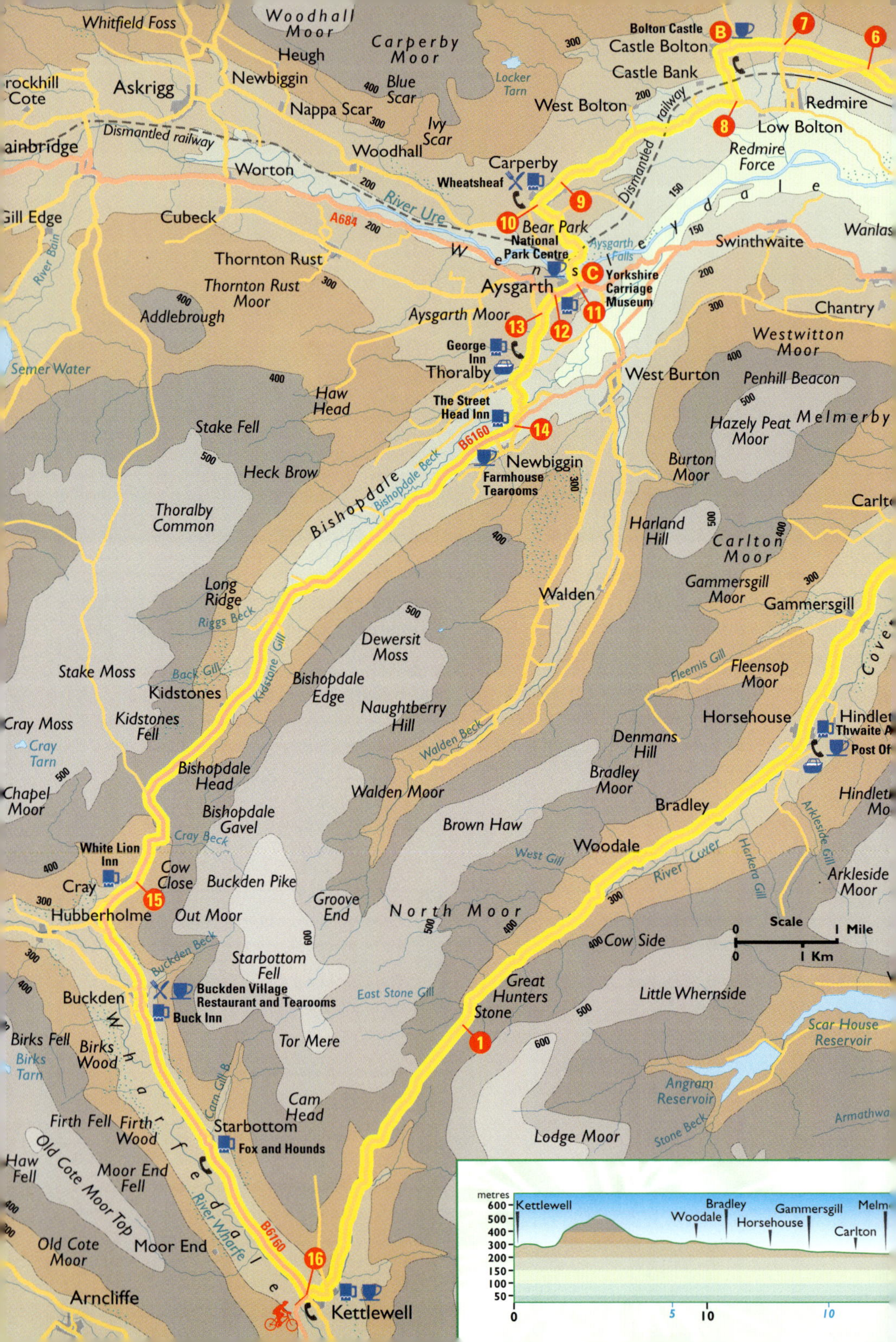
Whitfield Foss
Woodhall Moor
Carperby Moor
Bolton Castle
Castle Bolton
Castle Bank
Redmire
Low Bolton
Redmire Force
Askrigg
Heugh
Newbiggin
Blue Scar
Locker Tarn
Nappa Scar
Ivy Scar
West Bolton
Woodhall
Dismantled railway
Worton
Carperby
Wheatsheaf
River Ure
A684
Cubeck
Gill Edge
Bear Park
National Park Centre
Aysgarth Falls
Swinthwaite
Wanlass
Thornton Rust
Thornton Rust Moor
Aysgarth
Yorkshire Carriage Museum
Addlebrough
Aysgarth Moor
Chantry
River Bain
Semer Water
George Inn
Thoralby
Westwitton Moor
West Burton
Penhill Beacon
Haw Head
Stake Fell
The Street Head Inn
B6160
Hazely Peat Moor
Melmerby
Heck Brow
Bishopdale
Bishopdale Beck
Newbiggin
Farmhouse Tearooms
Burton Moor
Thoralby Common
Harland Hill
Carlton Moor
Long Ridge
Riggs Beck
Walden
Gammersgill Moor
Gammersgill
Dewersit Moss
Stake Moss
Back Gill
Kidstones
Kidstone Gill
Bishopdale Edge
Naughtberry Hill
Fleemis Gill
Fleensop Moor
Cray Moss
Kidstones Fell
Cray Tarn
Walden Beck
Horsehouse
Denmans Hill
Hindlethwaite
Thwaite Arms
Post Office
Bishopdale Head
Chapel Moor
Walden Moor
Bradley Moor
Bradley
Bishopdale Gavel
Brown Haw
Cray Beck
White Lion Inn
Cow Close
West Gill
Woodale
Arkleside Gill
Cray
Buckden Pike
River Cover
Arkleside Moor
Hubberholme
Out Moor
Groove End
North Moor
Cow Side
Scale
1 Mile
1 Km
Buckden Beck
Starbottom Fell
Buckden
Buckden Village Restaurant and Tearooms
Great Hunters Stone
Little Whernside
East Stone Gill
Buck Inn
Birks Fell
Birks Wood
Birks Tarn
Tor Mere
Scar House Reservoir
Angram Reservoir
Cam Gill B.
Cam Head
Firth Fell
Firth Wood
Starbottom
Fox and Hounds
Lodge Moor
Stone Beck
Old Cote Moor Top
Haw Fell
Moor End Fell
River Wharfe
Wharfedale
Old Cote Moor
Moor End
Arncliffe
Kettlewell
metres
Kettlewell
Woodale
Bradley
Horsehouse
Gammersgill
Carlton
Melmerby

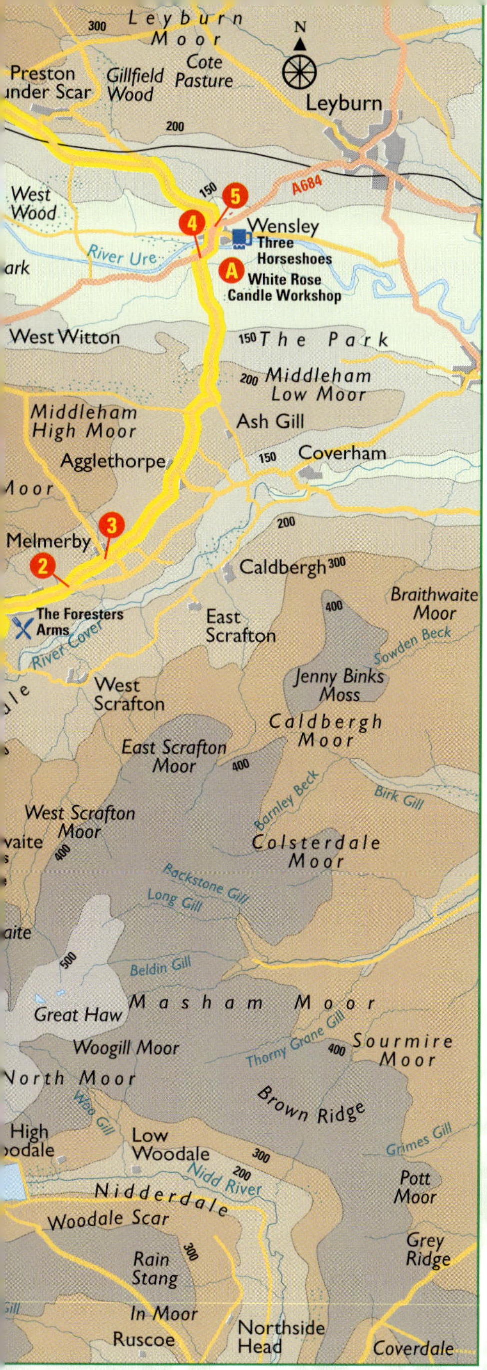

1 Reach top of the hill (4.5km/3 miles) and continue on road is it descends to Horsehouse (13.5km/8.5 miles). Continue through Horsehouse and on to Carlton

2 As leave Carton, TL SP Melmerby/Wensley/Leyburn. ***19km (12 miles)***

3 Follow road to right, SP Wensley/Leyburn, and descend towards Wensley.

4 TR at TJ, SP Wensley/Leyburn A684 (24km/15 miles) and cycle into Wensley. You will pass the Candle Workshop on the right.

5 TL, SP Castle Bolton/Aysgarth Falls/Preston/Redmire/Carperby.

6 SO at staggered XR (TR SP Catterick Camp/Richmond), along grass centred, gated single track road. ***29.5km (18.5 miles)***

7 SO at XR, SP Castle Bolton and continue through Castle Bolton, passing the castle on the right.

8 TR at TJ, SP Carperby/Aysgarth Falls/Askrigg.

9 Arrive Carperby and continue through village. ***35.5km (22 miles)***

10 At end of village, TL SP Aysgarth Falls/National Park. Continue, past the National Park Centre, across the bridge and pass the Yorkshire Carriage Museum on the left.

11 TR at TJ, SP Aysgarth/Bainbridge/Hawes. Pass several pubs and a tearoom.

12 TL, SP Thoralby.

13 TL at TJ, SP Thoralby, and cycle through the village. ***41km (25.5 miles)***

14 TR at TJ, SP Kettlewell/Skipton. Continue along this road through Bishopdale, passing pubs and a tearoom.

15 Cycle through Cray (51.5km/32 miles). Continue on this road, through the villages of Buckden and Starbottom, towards Kettlewell.

16 Arrive Kettlewell and finish the route at the bridge. ***60km (37.5 miles)***

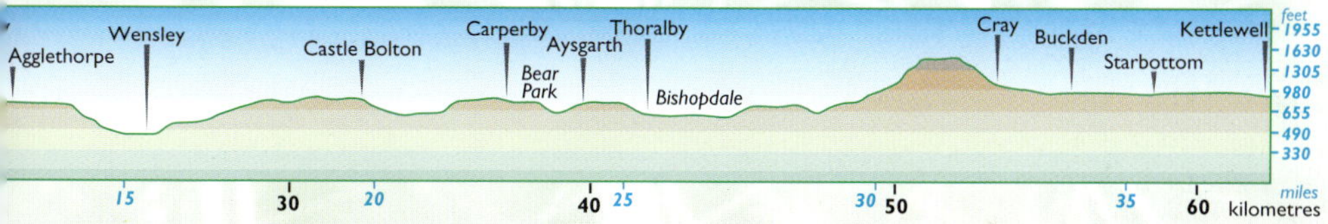

Route 18

RIPON LOOP – FOUNTAINS ABBEY AND RIPLEY CASTLE

Route information

Distance 64km (40 miles)

Grade Moderate

Terrain Quiet roads and lanes, with two sections of off-road track. Suitable for most bicycles.

Time to allow 5–8 hours.

Getting there by car Ripon is on the eastern side of the Yorkshire Dales, easily accessible by taking the A61 from the A1. There is long stay car parking close to the market place.

Getting there by train There is no practical railway access to this ride.

A long ride linking several beautiful attractions – take your time and enjoy some of them. From Ripon the route follows an easy bridleway towards Fountains Abbey. A series of lanes and a brief section of B road take you on a gentle descent, past the numerous formations of Brimham Rocks. Through Burnt Yates for a delightful piece of off-road, skirting the edge of Ripley Castle. The second section of the route passes through Scotton and Staveley to the old Roman town of Boroughbridge. The route finishes with some easy cycling through Skelton, back to Ripon.

Places of interest along the route

A Ripon

Ripon was granted its first charter by Alfred the Great in 886 AD and retains many Medieval and Georgian buildings. There have been several churches on the site of **Ripon Cathedral**. A monastery was built here in around 660 AD, and a little later the first church was built by St Wilfrid. Much of his building was destroyed by the Danes in the 9th century, but the crypt of the original Saxon church remains. A second church was built and this was destroyed by the Normans, who replaced it with a third church, some of which remains. Construction of the cathedral was begun in the 12th century and there has been much rebuilding over the centuries. Open all year, daily 0800–1845 (closing times may vary). Gift shop. Charge for guided tour, otherwise admission free. Telephone

Food and drink

There are lots of places for refreshment in Ripon, Ripley and Boroughbridge. Refreshments are also available at Fountains Abbey, Brimham Rocks and Ripley Castle. There are plenty of pubs along the route and a shop at Staveley and Skelton.

Guy Fawkes Inn, Scotton

Bar meals available. Closed Tuesday.

The Crown Inn, Farnham

Meals served at weekends only.

(01765) 603462. The **Police and Prison Museum** houses items concerned with local crime and punishment. Open daily, April and October, 1300–1600; May, June and September, 1300–1700; July and August, 1100–1700. Charge. Telephone (01765) 603006. **Ripon Workhouse Museum** is located in the old Victorian workhouse and is dedicated to the lives and treatment of the paupers who lived and worked here. Open April to June, September and October, daily 1300–1700; July and August, Monday–Saturday 1100–1700, Sunday 1300–1700. Charge. Telephone Ripon Tourist Information Centre for further information on (01765) 604625.

B Fountains Abbey and Studley Royal Water Garden, near Ripon

Fountains Abbey, the most complete remains of a Cistercian Abbey in Britain, and the landscaped gardens of Studley Royal were purchased by the National Trust in 1983. Designated a World Heritage Site, this is an idyllic place to visit. Restaurant and shop. Open daily, April to September 1000–1900; October to March 1000–1700. Admission charge, free guided tours. Telephone (01765) 608888 for further information.

C Brimham Rocks

Brimham Rocks are possibly one of the most peculiar rock formations in the country – 24ha (60 acres) of millstone grit rock, formed into weird and wonderful shapes by the elements. National Trust property. Site open at all reasonable times. Information centre, shop and refreshment kiosk open March, May and October, weekends and bank holidays, 1100–1700; June to September, daily 1100–1700. Free admission. Telephone (01904) 702021.

D Ripley Castle

The castle, deer park, lakes and woodland have been home to the same family for over 650 years. Guided tours of the castle; visitors can also wander through the park and gardens. Café. Castle open 1000–1500, gardens open 1000–1700: January to March, November and December, Tuesday, Thursday and weekends; April to June, September and October, Thursday, Friday and weekends; July and August, daily. Charge but free admission to café. Telephone (01423) 770152.

E Boroughbridge

There has been a settlement on this site since the Bronze Age. In around 72 AD the Romans built Isurium Brigantium (Aldborough), about 1.5km (1 mile) south east of the present town, where they could forge the River Ure. In the 11th century, the Normans moved the river crossing to the site of the present bridge and a settlement developed. The town was one of the busiest staging posts on the Great North road, with 22 inns. At **Aldborough Roman Town** visitors can see two spectacular mosaic pavements, the remaining sections of the massive town wall and its towers. Exhibition on the life of the Romans in Aldborough. English Heritage site. Open April to November, daily 1000–1300 and 1400–1800 (or dusk if earlier). Charge. Telephone English Heritage on (0171) 973 3434.

Route description

Starting from the Market Place in Ripon, cycle downhill along Kirkgate, SP Boroughbridge/ Pateley Bridge/Harrogate. TR at TJ, SP Pateley Bridge, onto the B6265 along Water Skellgate. TL at traffic lights, no SP. Continue along Low Skellgate, pass over bridge and into residential area.

1 TR opposite South Lodge pub, into Whitcliffe Lane, SP Cathedral Choir School. Pass residential houses.

2 As houses end, TL up single track road, SP Unsuitable for Motors. Pass Whitcliffe Farm on the left.

3 TR at top of hill, onto hardcore based track, no SP. Track goes downhill, then climbs again.

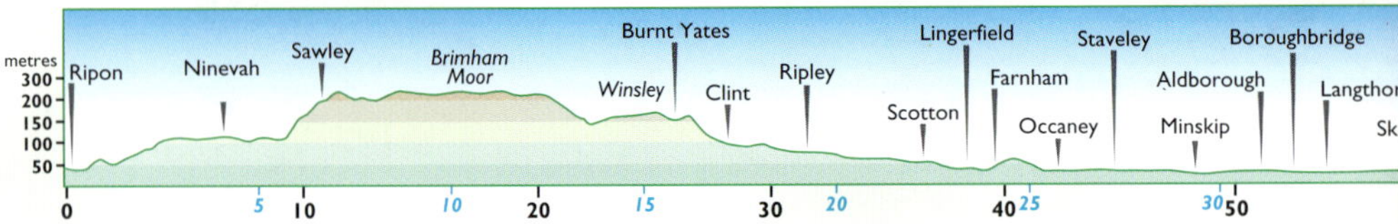

4 TR at TJ, no SP (6.5km/4 miles). Pass the Tower on the left (a distinctive church on a hill).

5 To visit Fountains Abbey, SO to the west entrance. Otherwise, TL, SP Sawley, and continue uphill along narrow hedged lane.

6 TR into Low Gate Lane, SP Single Track Road, and continue to Sawley.

7 TL at TJ opposite the Sawley Arms, no SP. ***10.5km (6.5 miles)***

8 TR into Sawley Moor Lane, SP Brimham Rocks/Pateley Bridge.

9 TL at TJ onto the B6265, SP Pateley Bridge/ Brimham Rocks.

10 TL, SP Brimham Rocks/Summer Bridge (15km/9.5 miles). Pass the entrance to Brimham Rocks on the right.

11 TL at XR, SP Burnt Yates/Harrogate/ Knaresborough. ***19km (12 miles)***

12 TL at TJ onto B6165, SP Knaresborough/ Harrogate. Cycle through Burnt Yates.

13 TR at XR, SP Birstwith/Hampsthwaite, along Clint Bank. ***25km (15.5 miles)***

14 TL, SP Clint/Hampsthwaite, and continue along Clint Bank Lane.

15 TL down track, SP Dead End. Continue through gate next to Hollybank Lodge and onto bridlepath. Follow SP Public Bridleway SO, keeping wall to the left. Ripley Castle appears on the left. Cross bridge and pass the entrance to Ripley Castle.

16 TR at TJ, SP London. ***30km (18.5 miles)***

17 SO at roundabout onto B6165, SP Knaresborough/Nidd Hall Hotel. Continue through Nidd.

18 TL, SP Scotton/Farnham (34km/21 miles). Cycle along Hawkskill Lane and through Scotton, Lingerfield and Farnham.

19 TL, SP Copgrove/Staveley, and continue into Staveley.

20 TL, SP Minskip/Boroughbridge. ***42km (26 miles)***

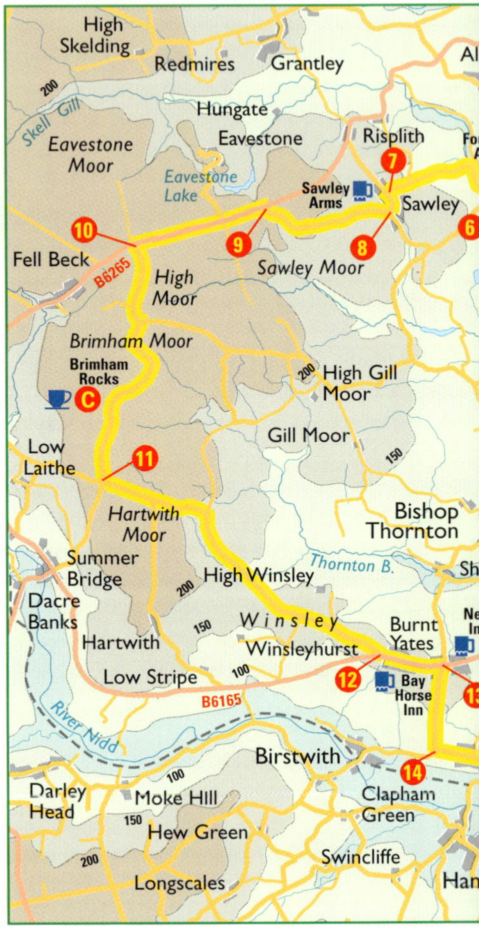

21 TL at TJ onto A6055, SP Boroughbridge.

22 SO at first roundabout, SP The North and South A1 (46.5km/29 miles); then SO at roundabout, SP Boroughbridge/Dishforth/the South/Wetherby; and SO at third roundabout, SP Boroughbridge.

23 TR, SP Aldborough Roman Town.

24 SO at XR, SP Aldborough. Pass the Roman town on the left.

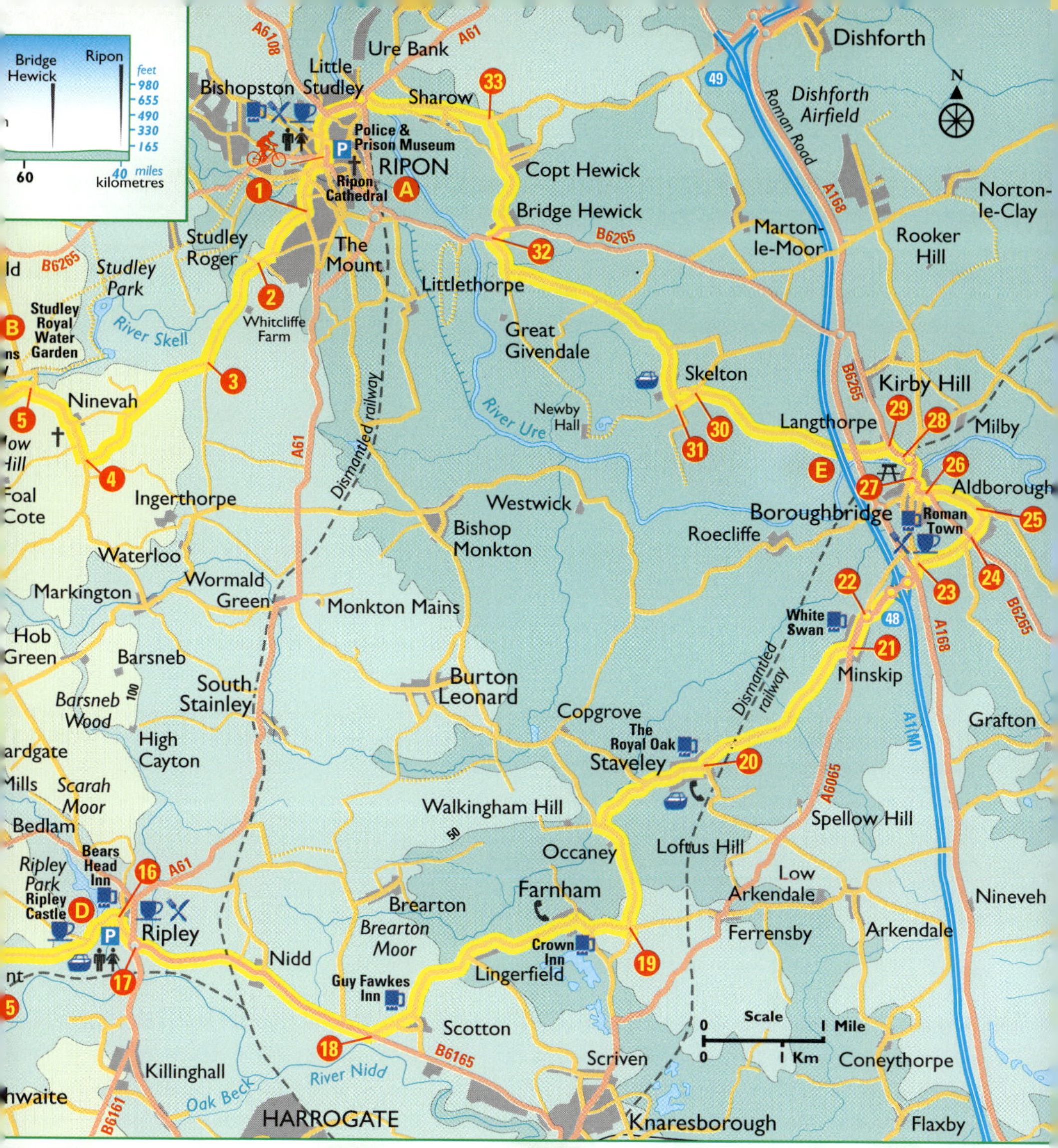

25 TL at TJ, no SP.

26 TR at TJ onto B6265, SP the North/the South. Arrive Boroughbridge Main Street.

27 TR at TJ, no SP, and continue over bridge.

28 TL at roundabout, SP the North/Ripon. Enter Langthorpe.

29 TL, SP Langthorpe/Skelton.
50.5km (31.5 miles)

30 TL, SP Newby Hall, along a drive towards gates.

31 TR opposite gates, no SP. Continue.
54km (33.5 miles)

32 TR at TJ onto B6265, SP Boroughbridge. TL, SP Copt Hewick. ***59km (36.5 miles)***

33 TL at TJ, SP Ripon. Cycle downhill through Sharow. SO at roundabout, onto A6108. Follow this road back to the centre of town and the end of the route. ***64km (40 miles)***

Route 19

GARGRAVE AND SLAIDBURN

Route information

Distance 66km (41 miles)

Grade Moderate

Terrain Mostly quiet, flat lanes with one climb and an undulating B road.

Time to allow 4–7 hours.

Getting there by car Gargrave is on the A65 Kendal to Skipton road. There is car parking in the village.

Getting there by train Gargrave Station is just outside the village. Telephone (0345) 484950 for timetable information.

This route heads west out of Gargrave, initially along the Leeds and Liverpool Canal, to the attractive village of Bolton by Bowland. A climb and descent into Slaidburn and then along the B6478 as it travels north east, with good views of the southern Dales. You enter the Yorkshire Dales National Park just after Hellifield and the flat terrain continues through the villages of Otterburn and Airton, before returning to Gargrave.

Places of interest along the route

A Gargrave

Gargrave is an attractive and much-visited village. It sits near the head of Airedale, between the Leeds and Liverpool Canal and the River Aire, which divides the village. The Leeds and Liverpool Canal is the longest single canal in the country at 204km (127 miles). Several ambitious trans-Pennine schemes were put forward before the canal was authorised in 1770. The section between Leeds and Gargrave was opened in 1777 and the canal became quite prosperous. However, the arrival of the railway, two world wars and the very hard winter of 1962–3 served to finish freight carriage on this waterway, which is now dedicated to the boater, cyclist and walker.

B Slaidburn

The moorland village of Slaidburn sits beside the River Hodder, on the edge of the Forest of Bowland. The village has retained its traditional village green, cobbled pavements and grey stone houses, some of the buildings dating from the 18th century. The pub has a curious name, the Hark to Bounty, and the pub sign is illustrated with a clergyman listening to a dog baying at the moon. The local story is that Bounty was a foxhound owned by an 18th-century parson, Wigglesworth. When Wigglesworth drank at the pub, he would leave the dog outside and, when it barked, would say 'Hark to Bounty'! The Slaidburn Heritage Centre offers information on local history. For opening hours and further information telephone (01200) 446161.

Leeds and Liverpool Canal

Food and drink

Gargrave has numerous places for food and drink and there are pubs in Bolton by Bowland, Wigglesworth and Hellifield. There are convenience stores in the villages throughout the route.

Tea Shop, Bolton by Bowland
Tearoom connected to the Post Office; also small information centre.

Hark to Bounty, Slaidburn
Village pub with a curious name.

Route description

From Gargrave, head towards the station and TR along Marton Road, pass under railway and over canal, following right bank. Continue through flat farmland. From Gargrave Station, TL out of station, towards Gargrave, TL along Marton Road and continue as above.

1 TR, SP Hellifield/Settle. Continue along hedged lane. ***4.5km (3 miles)***

2 TR at TJ onto A682, SP Hellifield/Settle.

3 TL, SP Halton West/Bolton by Bowland (11km/7 miles). Cycle through Halton West, following SP Bolton by Bowland, and into Bolton by Bowland.

4 TR at TJ, SP Clitheroe/Slaidburn (22km/13.5 miles). Cross the bridge.

5 TR, SP Holden/Slaidburn.

6 TL, SP Lane Ends. Climb.

7 Pass telephone on left and TR at TJ, SP Slaidburn. ***26km (16 miles)***

8 To visit Slaidburn, TL at TJ, SP Slaidburn/Trough of Bowland, and descend into village (29.5km/18.5 miles). After visit, retrace your route and continue on the B6478, all the way past Wigglesworth. Otherwise, TR onto B6478 and continue.

9 Cross bridge and immediately TR into a narrow lane, SP Hellifield. ***48km (30 miles)***

10 TR at TJ, no SP.

11 TL down a very narrow lane, no SP (51km/31.5 miles). Enter Hellifield.

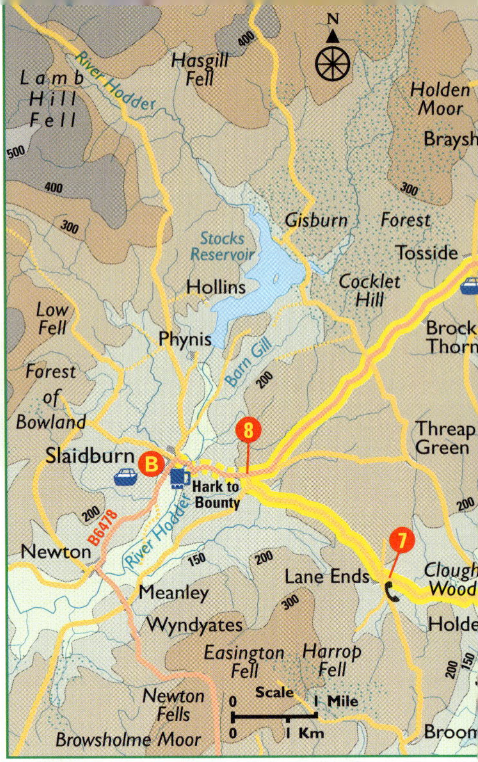

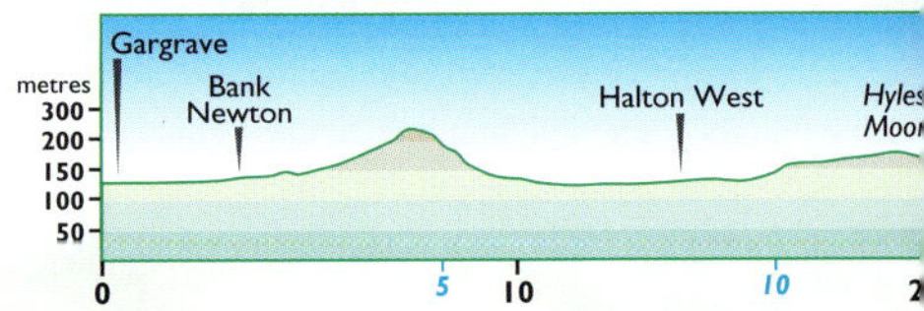

12 Cycle under railway bridge and TL at TJ, no SP. Pass the Black Horse pub on the left.

13 TR at TJ onto the A65, SP Skipton/Gargrave/Malham.

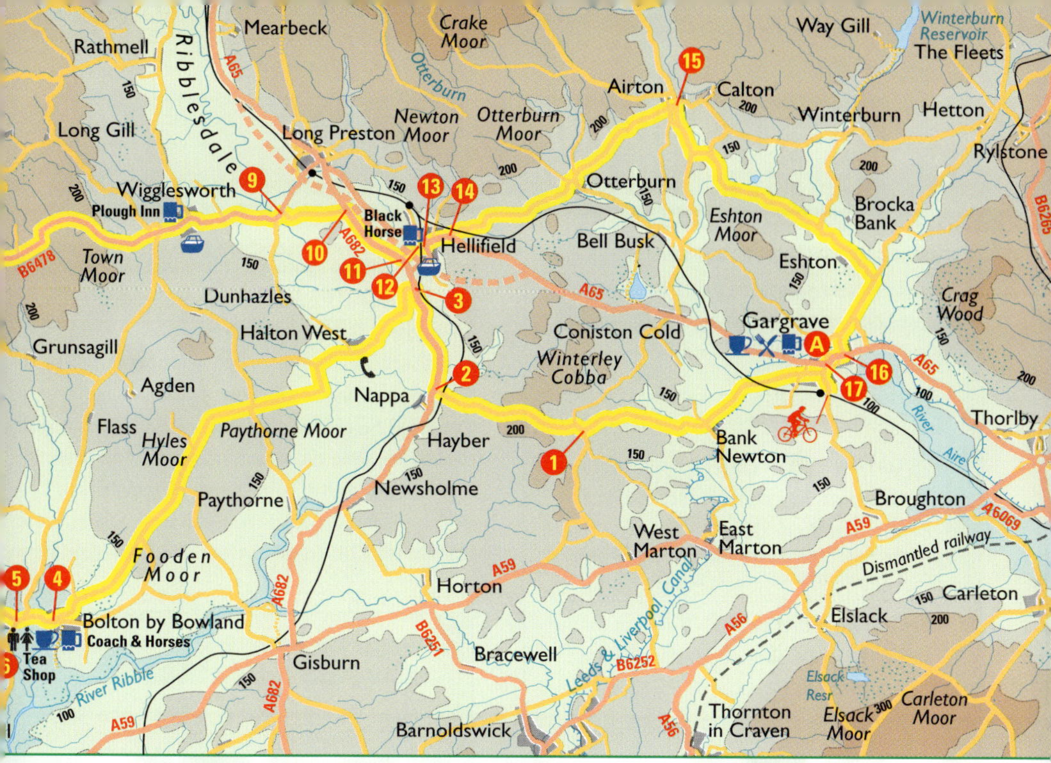

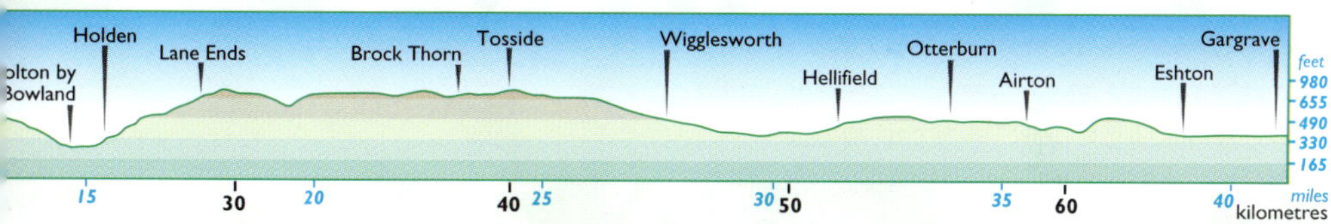

14 TL, SP Airton/Malham. Continue through Otterburn and on to Airton.

15 TR at XR, SP Bell Busk/Gargrave (58km/ 36 miles). Follow SP to Gargrave. Enter village.

16 TR at TJ, SP Kendal.

17 TL, SP Station. Cross the bridge and return to the station and the end of the route.

66km (41 miles)

Route 20

REETH AND THE BUTTERTUBS PASS

Route information

Distance 67.5km (42 miles)

Grade Strenuous

Terrain This route takes in four Dales, so there are plenty of hills, some of them steep.

Time to allow 4–7 hours.

Getting there by car Reeth is on the B6270 in Swaledale, to the north of the Yorkshire Dales. There is car parking around the large village green.

Getting there by train There is no practical railway access to this ride.

Along Swaledale from Reeth, the route crosses the River Swale at Gunnerside. A steep, gated road leads to a fast descent into Askrigg and heads west through Wensleydale. Over the Buttertubs Pass and up beautiful West Stones Dale, full of traditional Dales stone barns. On up to the highest pub in England, at Tan Hill, and then a steady descent along Arkengarthdale, back into Reeth.

Places of interest along the route

A Reeth

The village of Reeth is strategically sited at the junctions of Swaledale and Arkengarthdale, the most northerly of the Yorkshire Dales. There is a large village green, which is still the focal point of many traditional events. Market day is on Friday. The folk museum, craft workshops and tearooms make Reeth a popular place to visit. The **Swaledale Folk Museum** illustrates the local history of the Dales – village life and traditions, religion, farming, mining and knitting, and much more. Gift shop. Open Easter to October, daily 1030–1700. Charge. Telephone (01748) 884373. Local crafts have played a large

Food and drink

Plenty of choice in Reeth and pubs along the route. There is a shop in Gunnerside and Langthwaite.

Ghyll Foot Tearoom, Gunnerside
Food served all day.

The Game Tavern, Hardraw
Bar meals, and tea and coffee served.

Kearton Tea Shop, Thwaite
Lovely tearoom with a large window at one end for a view of the Dales.

Tan Hill Inn, Tan Hill
England's highest pub at 528m (1732 feet). Morning coffee, bar snacks and meals served. A welcome sight indeed, once you have reached the top of the hill.

Chapel Farm Tearoom, Whaw
Follow the turn for Whaw for 600m downhill. Morning coffee and afternoon tea.

CB Inn, Arkengarthdale
Eighteenth-century bar and restaurant.

part in the life of the Dales and today's craft-workers continue the tradition of producing high quality goods. Located in the **Dales Centre** in Reeth, are the workshops of a cabinet maker (01748) 884555, guitar maker (01748) 884887, clock maker (01748) 884088, artists' studio ((01748) 884663 as well as animal modelling (01748) 884498 and rug making (01748) 884435. Opening times of individual workshops vary, so please telephone to confirm.

B Buttertubs Pass

The Buttertubs Pass lies between Hardraw and Muker and is an exhilarating 526m (1726 feet) above sea level. The Buttertubs themselves are four deep holes in the limestone.

Route description

From the Tourist Information Centre in Reeth, cycle up the hill (with the tearooms and pubs to the left and the green to the right). At the top, TL at TJ onto B6270, SP Craft Workshops/ Reeth Bakery. Pass the Dales Centre on the right. Follow the road along Swaledale, through Healaugh, Low Row (5.5km/3.5 miles) and Gunnerside where you cross the River Swale, following SP for Muker.

Gunnerside, Swaledale

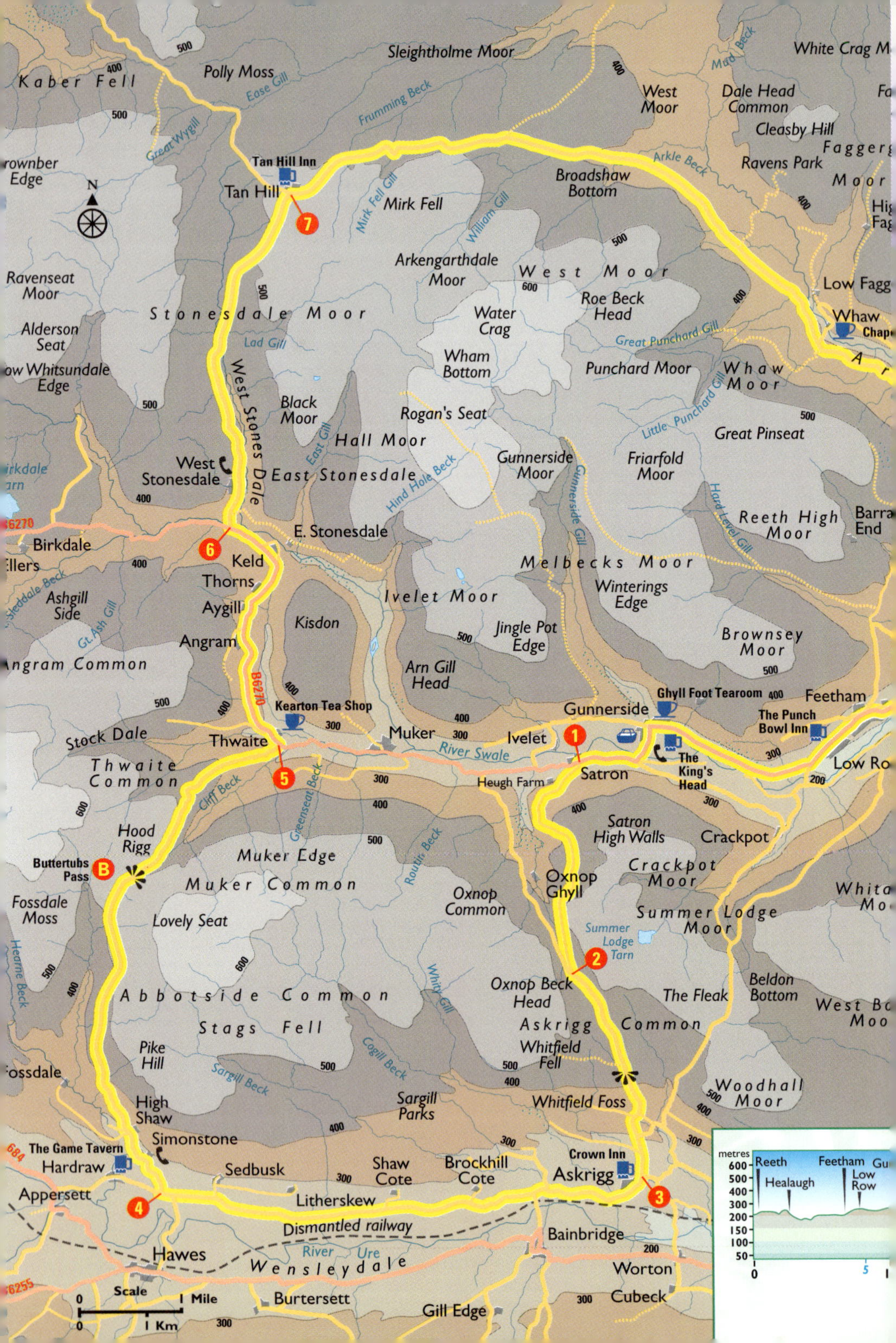
Sleightholme Moor
Polly Moss
Kaber Fell
Ease Gill
Frumming Beck
Mud Beck
White Crag Moor
West Moor
Dale Head Common
Cleasby Hill
Faggergill Moor
Great Wygill
Tan Hill Inn
Tan Hill
7
Mirk Fell Gill
Mirk Fell
William Gill
Broadshaw Bottom
Arkle Beck
Ravens Park
Crownber Edge
N
Ravenseat Moor
Arkengarthdale Moor
West Moor
Roe Beck Head
Low Faggergill
Whaw
Stonesdale Moor
Water Crag
Great Punchard Gill
Alderson Seat
Lad Gill
Wham Bottom
Punchard Moor
Whaw Moor
Low Whitsundale Edge
West Stones Dale
Black Moor
Rogan's Seat
Little Punchard Gill
Great Pinseat
East Gill
Hall Moor
Gunnerside Moor
Friarfold Moor
West Stonesdale
East Stonesdale
Hind Hole Beck
Gunnerside Gill
Hard Level Gill
Reeth High Moor
Barras End
B6270
E. Stonesdale
Birkdale
6
Keld
Melbecks Moor
Thorns
Winterings Edge
Ashgill Side
Aygill
Ivelet Moor
Kisdon
Gt. Ash Gill
Jingle Pot Edge
Brownsey Moor
Angram
Angram Common
Arn Gill Head
B6270
Ghyll Foot Tearoom
Feetham
Kearton Tea Shop
Gunnerside
The Punch Bowl Inn
Stock Dale
Muker
Ivelet
1
Thwaite
River Swale
The King's Head
Low Row
Thwaite Common
Cliff Beck
5
Greenseat Beck
Heugh Farm
Satron
Satron High Walls
Crackpot
Hood Rigg
Muker Edge
Routin Beck
Buttertubs Pass
B
Muker Common
Oxnop Ghyll
Crackpot Moor
Fossdale Moss
Oxnop Common
Summer Lodge Moor
Lovely Seat
Summer Lodge Tarn
2
Hearne Beck
Whitaside Moor
Abbotside Common
Oxnop Beck Head
Whitty Gill
The Fleak
Beldon Bottom
Askrigg Common
West Bolton Moor
Stags Fell
Pike Hill
Cogill Beck
Whitfield Fell
Fossdale
Sargill Beck
Woodhall Moor
High Shaw
Sargill Parks
Whitfield Foss
Simonstone
The Game Tavern
Crown Inn
Hardraw
Sedbusk
Shaw Cote
Brockhill Cote
Askrigg
3
Appersett
4
Litherskew
Dismantled railway
Bainbridge
Hawes
River Ure
Wensleydale
Worton
B6255
Scale
0
1 Mile
0
1 Km
Burtersett
Gill Edge
Cubeck
metres
600
500
400
300
200
150
100
50
Reeth
Healaugh
Feetham
Low Row
0
5

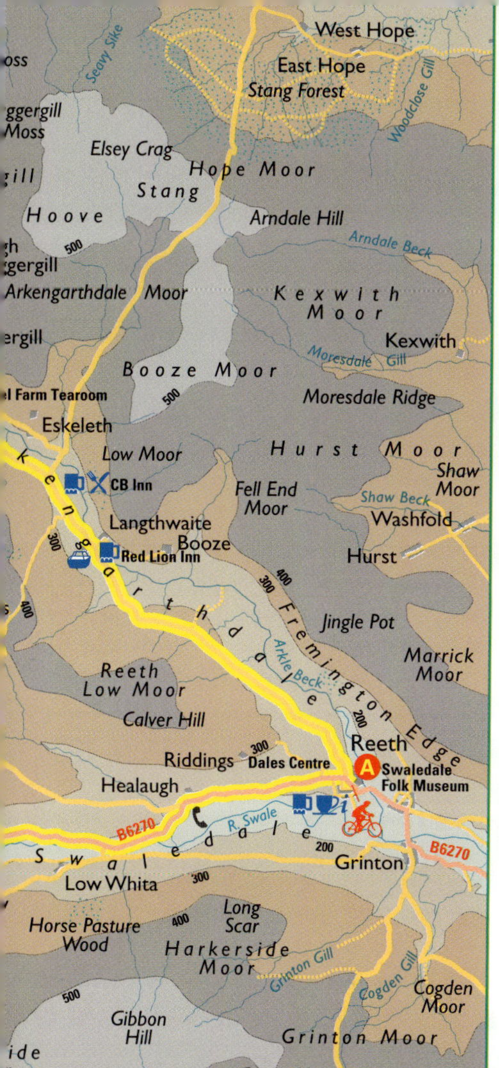

1 Shortly after the bridge, TL in the unmarked hamlet of Satron (12km/7.5 miles). There is no SP except one in green pointing to Heugh Farm B&B. Climb sharply for 400m and pass through a gate. Pass Heugh Farm on the right and continue to climb the gated road that is rough in places.

2 TL at TJ (effectively SO), no SP (16km/10 miles). Cross a cattle grid and descend quickly into Askrigg.

3 TR at TJ, SP Hawes (20km/12.5 miles). Leave Askrigg and continue towards Hardraw.

4 TR, SP Muker via Buttertubs/Simonstone (28.5km/17.5 miles). Pass SP 1 in 6 gradient and climb, crossing cattle grids. This beautiful road falls away steeply into the dale below. A lovely view along Swaledale develops as you descend to Muker.

5 TL at TJ, SP Keld/Kirkby Stephen (37.5km/23.5 miles). Go through Thwaite and climb, passing Keld.

6 TR, SP West Stonesdale/Tan Hill (42.5km/26.5 miles). Immediately start a hard but short zig-zagged climb up to Tan Hill.

7 TR at TJ, no SP (50.5km/31.5 miles). Pass the Tan Hill Inn on the left. Continue over open moorland, gradually descending. Pass Whaw and continue through Langthwaite (62.5km/39 miles). Cross another cattle grid and enter another stretch of open moorland (for 3.5km/2 miles). Arrive Reeth and the end of the route.

67.5km (42 miles)

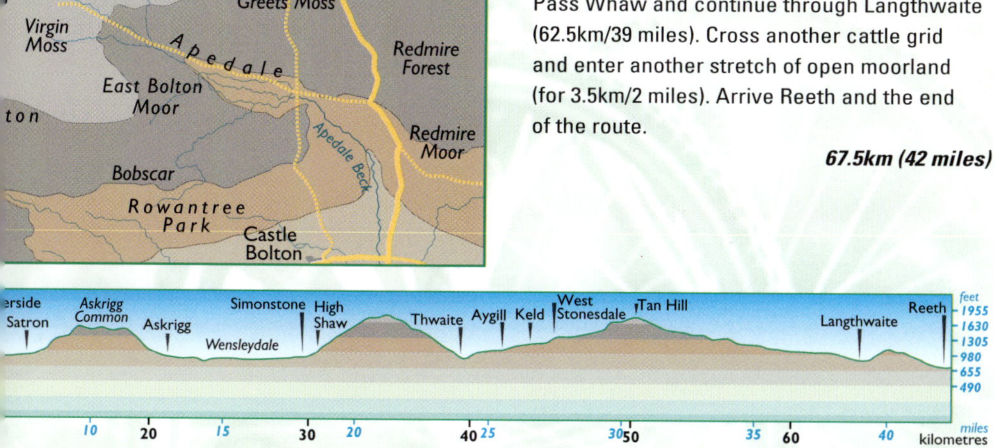

Route 21

HARROGATE, PATELEY BRIDGE AND OTLEY

Route information

Distance 71km (44 miles)

Grade Strenuous

Terrain Tarmac roads and a few steep climbs.

Time to allow 5–8 hours.

Getting there by car Harrogate is on the A61, to the south east of the Yorkshire Dales. There is plenty of long term car parking in the town.

Getting there by train There is a railway station in Harrogate. Telephone (0345) 484950 for timetable information.

Starting from the centre of Harrogate, this route heads north west along Nidderdale. Although this area is more built up than that north of Pateley Bridge, there are some pretty views of the River Nidd as you pass through the many villages that line its banks. From Pateley Bridge, the route to Otley is across sections of open moorland with extensive views. This is the hardest part of the route with several steep climbs. A series of quiet lanes take you through undulating countryside from Otley to Harrogate, before a final stretch of busier roads back into Harrogate.

Places of interest along the route

A Harrogate

Harrogate was well known as a spa town and still retains the original 19th-century **Turkish Baths**, in Crescent Road. The recommended visit time is 2½ hours, to enjoy the steam room, plunge pool and hot rooms. Open all year round, telephone for times on (01423) 562498. Charge. The **Pump Room Museum**, Crown Place, explains the history of Harrogate as a spa town. Open April to October, Monday–Saturday 1000–1700, Sunday 1400–1700. Charge. Telephone (01423) 503340. **Mercer Art Gallery**, Swan Road, is home to Harrogate District's collection of fine art. Open all year, Tuesday–Saturday 1000–1700. Admission free. Telephone (01423) 503340. **Harlow Carr Botanical Gardens** comprise 27.5ha (68 acres) of landscaped gardens, with glass houses, woodland trails, streams and waterfalls. Museum of Gardening, gift shop, plant centre, restaurant and refreshment kiosk. Open all year, daily 0930–1800 (or dusk if earlier). Charge. Telephone (01423) 565418.

B Yorkshire Country Wines, Glasshouses

Manufacturer of traditional fruit wines, in a 19th-century flax mill. Winery tours, tastings. Also antique furniture, paintings and ceramics for sale. Tearoom. Open May to September, Wednesday–Sunday 1130–1630; October to April, Saturday and Sunday 1130–1630; tours on Friday and Saturday at 1145. Telephone to confirm opening, as hours may vary. Charge for tours only. Telephone (01423) 711947.

C Nidderdale Museum, Pateley Bridge

Nidderdale, the valley of the River Nidd, stretches from Ripley in the south east, to the river's source in the north west, on Great Whernside. The award-winning Nidderdale Museum illustrates all aspects of local life and history. Displays include, among others, a cobbler's shop, general store, Victorian parlour, kitchen and schoolroom. There are exhibitions on agriculture, religion, industries, transport and costume. Open April–September, daily 1400–1700; October–March, Sunday only 1400–1700. Charge. Telephone (01423) 711225 for information.

Moorland

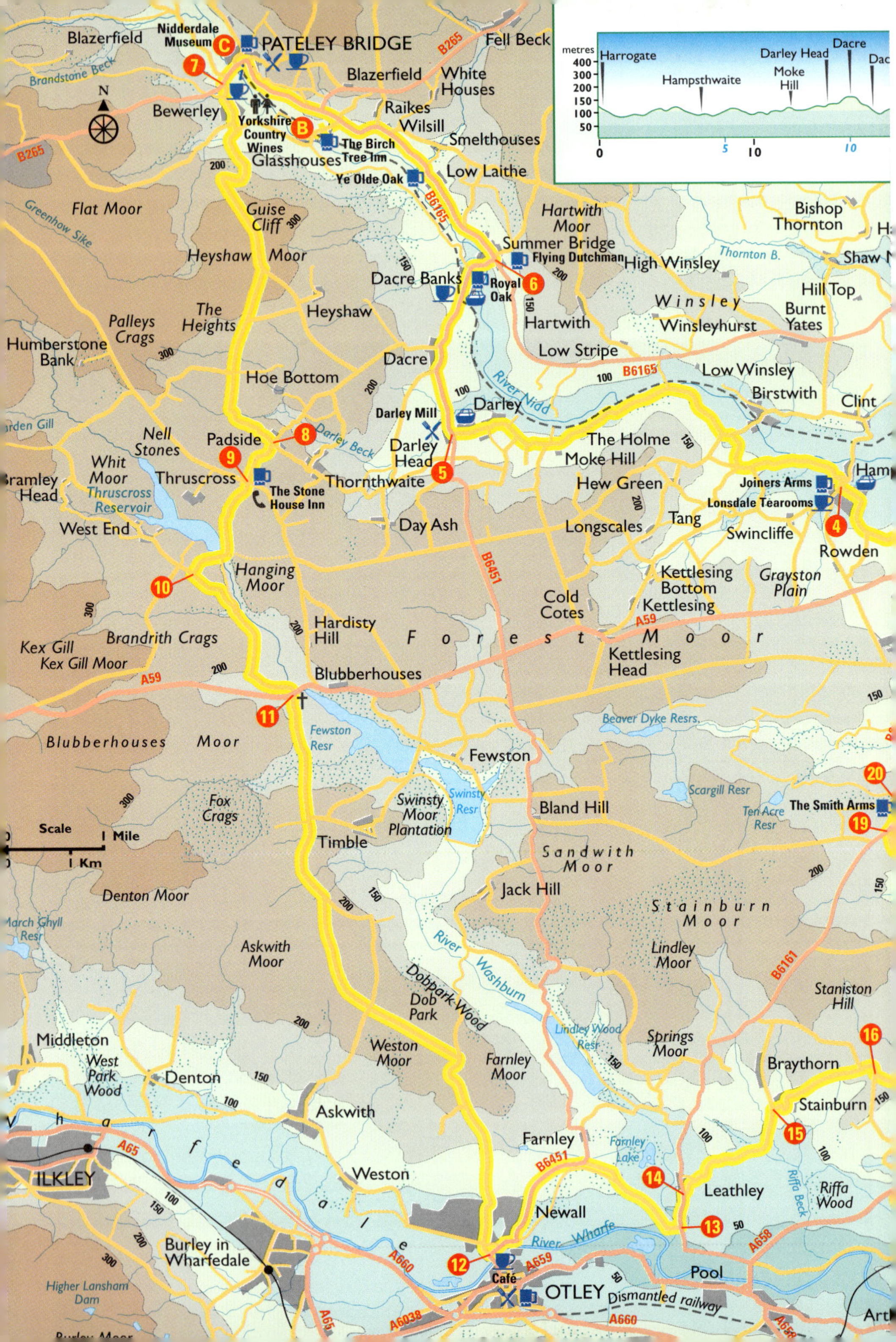
metres
400
300
200
150
100
50
0
5
10
10
Harrogate
Hampsthwaite
Darley Head
Moke Hill
Dacre
Blazerfield
Nidderdale Museum
C
PATELEY BRIDGE
B265
Fell Beck
7
Brandstone Beck
Blazerfield
White Houses
N
Bewerley
Raikes
Wilsill
Yorkshire Country Wines
B
The Birch Tree Inn
Smelthouses
B265
Glasshouses
200
Ye Olde Oak
Low Laithe
Greenhow Sike
Flat Moor
Guise Cliff
300
B6165
Hartwith Moor
Bishop Thornton
Summer Bridge
Flying Dutchman
High Winsley
Thornton B.
Shaw
Heyshaw
Moor
150
200
Dacre Banks
Royal Oak
6
Winsley
Hill Top
150
Burnt Yates
Palleys Crags
The Heights
Heyshaw
Hartwith
Winsleyhurst
Humberstone Bank
300
Low Stripe
Dacre
Hoe Bottom
200
100
B6165
Low Winsley
River Nidd
Birstwith
Clint
100
Darley Mill
Darley
Gill
Nell Stones
Padside
8
Darley Beck
The Holme
150
9
Darley Head
Moke Hill
Whit Moor
Bramley Head
Thruscross Reservoir
Thruscross
The Stone House Inn
Thornthwaite
5
Hew Green
Joiners Arms
Lonsdale Tearooms
200
Tang
4
West End
Day Ash
Longscales
Swincliffe
Rowden
Hanging Moor
B6451
Kettlesing Bottom
Grayston Plain
10
Cold Cotes
Kettlesing
300
A59
Hardisty Hill
Forest Moor
200
Kex Gill
Brandrith Crags
Kettlesing Head
Kex Gill Moor
A59
200
Blubberhouses
150
11
Fewston Resr
Beaver Dyke Resrs.
Blubberhouses Moor
Fewston
20
300
Swinsty Moor Plantation
Swinsty Resr
Scargill Resr
Fox Crags
Bland Hill
Ten Acre Resr
The Smith Arms
19
Scale
1 Mile
1 Km
Timble
Sandwith Moor
200
200
150
Denton Moor
150
Jack Hill
Stainburn Moor
March Ghyll Resr
Askwith Moor
River Washburn
Dobpark Wood
Dob Park
Lindley Moor
B6161
Staniston Hill
200
Lindley Wood Resr
150
Springs Moor
16
Middleton
Weston Moor
Farnley Moor
Braythorn
West Park Wood
Denton
150
100
Stainburn
150
Askwith
15
Wharfedale
A65
Farnley
Farnley Lake
100
100
ILKLEY
B6451
14
Weston
Riffa Beck
Leathley
Riffa Wood
100
150
Newall
13
50
River Wharfe
A658
200
Burley in Wharfedale
12
A659
A660
Café
Pool
300
OTLEY
Dismantled railway
50
Higher Lansham Dam
A65
A6038
A660
A658

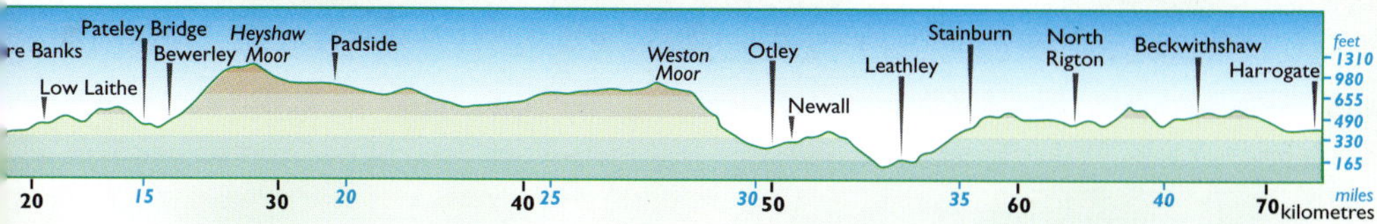

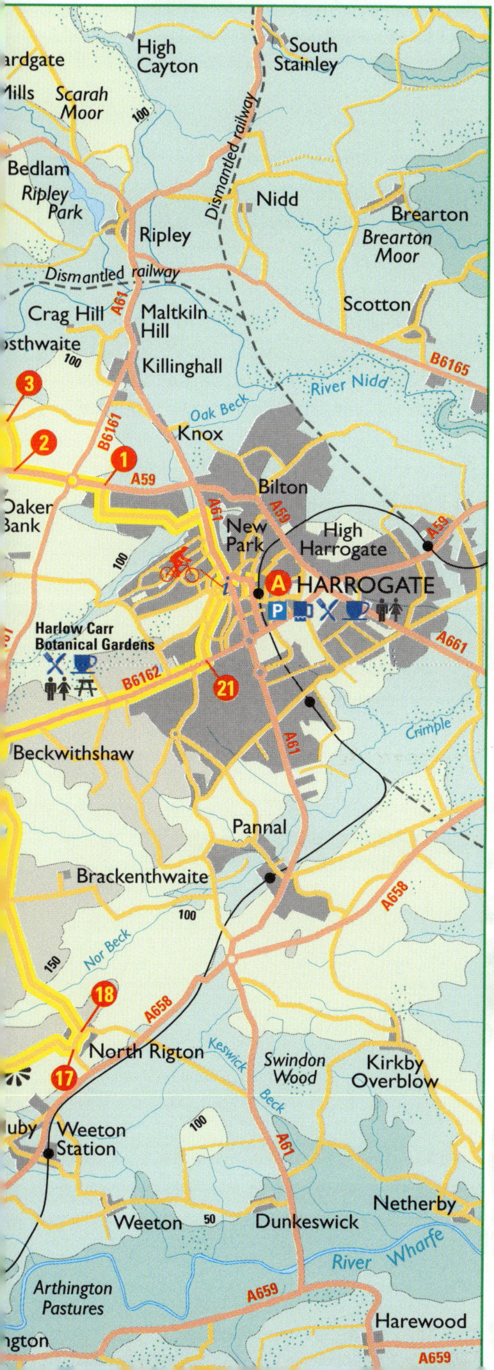

Route description

If starting the route from railway station, TR out of the station. TL and TR at traffic lights opposite the Tourist Information Centre, onto the A61, SP Ripon. Continue route as below. Otherwise, start at the front of the Tourist Information Centre and head for the nearest set of traffic lights (20m). TL at lights along the A61, SP Ripon. Pass the Majestic Hotel on the right. At second set of lights, TL into Jennyfield Road, along this residential street and TR into Crowberry Drive.

1 TL at TJ, no SP, then SO at the roundabout, SP Skipton.

2 TR, SP Hampsthwaite.

3 TL at TJ, SP Hampsthwaite/Birstwith (5km/3 miles). Continue along Hollins Lane and into Hampsthwaite.

4 TR at TJ, SP Birstwith/Darley. Bear left to follow River Nidd along Nidderdale. Pass through Birstwith and Darley ***14km (8.5 miles)***

5 TR at TJ onto B6451, SP Summer Bridge/ Pateley Bridge (15km/9.5 miles). Continue through Dacre and into Dacre Banks.

6 TL at TJ, SP Pateley Bridge/Ripon (18.5km/11.5 miles). Cycle through Low Laithe and Glasshouses (where pass entrance to Yorkshire Country Wines on left). Continue on this road as it descends into Pateley Bridge, where pass shops and Tourist Information Centre and cross the bridge.

7 Just before the road climbs steeply, TL, SP Bewerley Park Centre/Glasshouses (25km/ 15.5 miles). Continue on this road, climbing. Pass SP for Otley and climb again across moorland.

8 TR at XR, SP Otley/Skipton/Harrogate. ***33km (20.5 miles)***

9 SO at XR, SP West End. Descend and cross the dam of Thruscross Reservoir.

10 TL at TJ, SP Blubberhouses/Otley/ Harrogate. ***36km (22.5 miles)***

11 SO at XR, SP Otley (39km/24 miles). Pass church on left. Continue on this road for another climb, then cross moorland with views of Ilkley and Otley. Descend into Otley.

12 Just before crossing bridge into main part of Otley, TL along Farnley Lane (49.5km/ 31 miles). Pass Wrenbeck Drive on left and leave Otley. Bear right (effectively SO), leaving B6451.

13 TL at TJ, SP Killinghall/Ripon/Harrogate. ***54.5km (34 miles)***

14 TR, SP Stainburn, and cycle along a country lane.

15 TR, SP Huby/Rigton. Pass through the small hamlet of Stainburn.

16 TL, SP North Rigton. ***59.5 km (37 miles)***

17 TL at TJ, SP North Rigton.

18 TL at TJ, SP Beckwithshaw. Climb then descend.

19 TR at TJ, SP Killinghall/Harrogate/Ripon. ***66km (41 miles)***

20 TR on the B6162, SP Harrogate/ Knaresborough. Pass Harlow Carr Botanical Gardens on the left. Arrive Harrogate.

21 TL into Cold Bath Road. This descends to meet a roundabout where SO, SP Parking/Low Harrogate, to return to the Tourist Information Centre and the end of the route. ***71km (44 miles)***

Food and drink

Lots of places for refreshment in Harrogate, Pateley Bridge and Otley. There are pubs, stores and tearooms in Hampsthwaite, Dacre Banks, and a pub in Summer Bridge, Low Laithe, Glass-houses, near Padside and Beckwith-shaw. Refreshments also available at Harlow Carr Botanical Gardens and Yorkshire Country Wines.

Darley Mill, Darley Head
Restaurant with waterwheel.

Café, Otley
A popular stop for cyclists – café outside newsagent, just over bridge.

River Nidd, near Pateley Bridge

Route 22

WHARFEDALE – ILKLEY TO KETTLEWELL

Route information

Distance 80.5km (50 miles)

Grade Moderate

Terrain An optional steep climb at the start, followed by a mix of flat and undulating quiet lanes and moderately busy B roads.

Time to allow 5–8 hours.

Getting there by car Ilkley is on the A65, in the south east of the Yorkshire Dales. There is long stay car parking in the centre of town.

Getting there by train Ilkley is on the Leeds Metro line. Telephone (0345) 484950 for further information.

This route covers the length of Wharfedale, one of Yorkshire's prettiest dales. Starting from Ilkley, you cross the River Wharfe and head north towards Bolton Abbey, where the river is crossed again. The quieter easterly edge of Wharfedale is cycled, as you pass through the lovely communities of Appletreewick, Hebden and Grassington. At Kettlewell you descend along the busier western edge of the dale, with a rewarding spur to Arncliffe. Back through Burnsall and Barden and on to Bolton Abbey, with a flat section back to Ilkley.

Route description

Start at Ilkley Town Hall, opposite the train and bus stations. Cycle towards the centre of town where TR, SP Manor House. Pass the Yorkshire and Barclays Bank and the long stay car park on the left.

1 SO at XR (traffic lights) to cross A65, SP Middleton. Pass church on left and gently descend. Cross River Wharfe.

2 TL at XR into Denton Road, no SP (telephone to right of junction). The road is flat and then climbs. (To avoid the climb, take second TL into Nesfield Road and continue on this road, alongside River Wharfe to direction 4, where TL at TJ.) Otherwise, continue climbing, pass a large statue of Jesus on the cross on the left, then Windsover Farm on the right. Cross cattle grid and continue on single track, twisty road with excellent views, following SP for Bolton Abbey. At 7km (4.5 miles) take care on sharp descent. Cross another cattle grid.

3 TR at TJ, no SP but seat on left (9km/ 5.5 miles). Pass Home Farm and then telephone on left.

4 TL at TJ onto A59, SP Skipton. Almost immediately, TL onto cycle track, SP Bolton Abbey (blue SP). Pass under road bridge to meet old bridge where:

5 TL at TJ across old bridge, SP Bolton Bridge.

6 TR at TJ onto B6160, no SP (10.5km/ 6.5 miles). Pass telephone, National Park sign and then Bolton Abbey car park on left. Continue through distinctive arch.

12km (7.5 miles)

7 TR by the Cavendish Memorial, SP Riverside Car Park. Descend private road, past the ticket hut, cross the wooden bridge opposite the Cavendish Pavilion and cycle along the gravel track.

---

8 TL at TJ, no SP, and climb two steep hills (River Wharfe to left). Continue along the undulating single track road. Pass Holme House Farm on left.

---

9 TR at TJ (effectively SO), no SP (16.5km/10.5 miles). Pass Gamsworth Farm on left and telephone on right (by entrance to Howgill Lodge).

---

10 TL at TJ, SP Appletreewick (19.5km/12 miles). Continue through Appletreewick.

---

11 TR, SP Hartlington Raikes/Hebden, and climb steep hill.

---

12 TL, SP Hebden. Cycle along walled, single lane track into Hebden.

---

13 TL at TJ onto B6265, SP Grassington/Skipton (25.5km/16 miles). Continue into Grassington (Upper Wharfedale Folk Museum in centre of town).

---

14 TR, SP Conistone/Kettlewell. Pass SP Unsuitable for HGVs/Coaches. The road flattens out and the valley widens. Continue into Conistone.

---

15 TR by the maypole in the centre of Conistone, no SP (30.5km/19 miles). Pass church on left and cycle a narrow walled lane. Kilnsey Crag can be seen on the other side of the valley. Continue into Kettlewell.

---

16 TR by the seats and maypole in the centre of Kettlewell, SP Leyburn/Gradient 25%.

36km (22.5 miles)

---

17 TL at XR by shop, no SP. Pass Corner Shop Tearoom on left.

---

18 TL at TJ opposite Racehorses Hotel, SP Burnsall B6160/Skipton B6265. Cross the bridge. Continue.

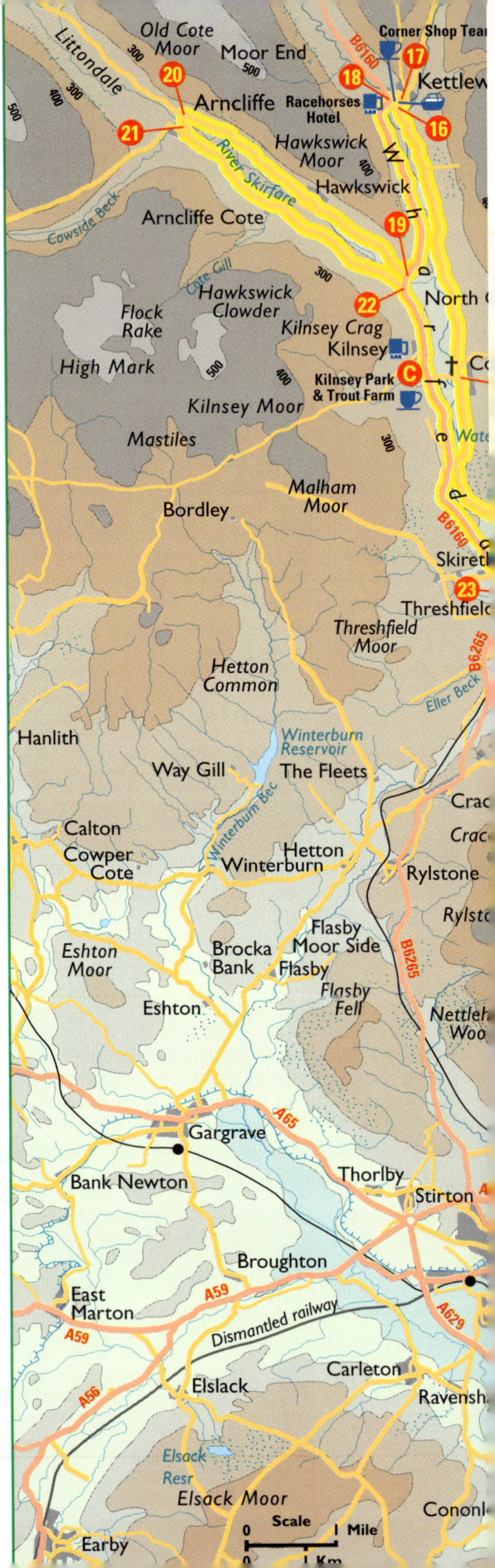

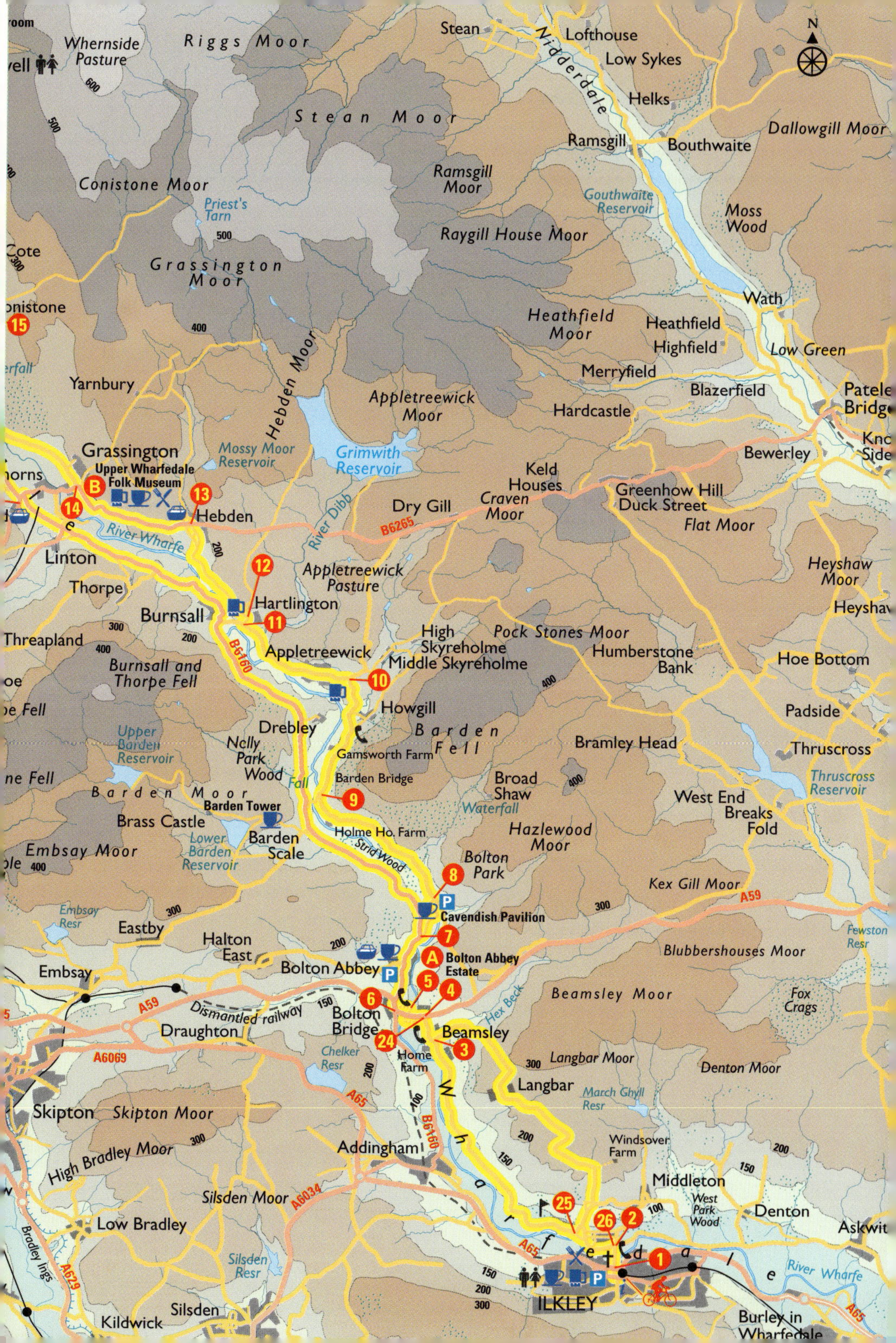

Whernside Pasture
Riggs Moor
Stean
Lofthouse
Low Sykes
Nidderdale
Helks
Stean Moor
Ramsgill
Bouthwaite
Dallowgill Moor
Conistone Moor
Priest's Tarn
Ramsgill Moor
Gouthwaite Reservoir
Moss Wood
Raygill House Moor
Grassington Moor
Wath
Heathfield Moor
Heathfield
Highfield
Low Green
Yarnbury
Merryfield
Blazerfield
Pateley Bridge
Hebden Moor
Appletreewick Moor
Hardcastle
Grassington
Upper Wharfedale Folk Museum
Mossy Moor Reservoir
Grimwith Reservoir
Keld Houses
Bewerley
Greenhow Hill
Duck Street
Hebden
Dry Gill
Craven Moor
Flat Moor
River Wharfe
River Dibb
B6265
Linton
Thorpe
Appletreewick Pasture
Heyshaw Moor
Burnsall
Hartlington
Threapland
Appletreewick
High Skyreholme
Middle Skyreholme
Pock Stones Moor
Humberstone Bank
Hoe Bottom
Burnsall and Thorpe Fell
B6160
Howgill
Barden Fell
Padside
Upper Barden Reservoir
Drebley
Nelly Park Wood
Gamsworth Farm
Bramley Head
Thruscross
Barden Bridge
Broad Shaw
Thruscross Reservoir
Barden Moor
Barden Tower
Waterfall
West End
Breaks Fold
Brass Castle
Lower Barden Reservoir
Barden Scale
Holme Ho. Farm
Strid Wood
Hazlewood Moor
Embsay Moor
Bolton Park
Kex Gill Moor
A59
Embsay Resr
Eastby
Cavendish Pavilion
Fewston Resr
Halton East
Bolton Abbey
Bolton Abbey Estate
Blubberhouses Moor
Embsay
Dismantled railway
Beamsley Moor
Fox Crags
Draughton
Bolton Bridge
Hex Beck
Beamsley
Home Farm
A6069
Chelker Resr
Langbar Moor
Denton Moor
A65
Langbar
March Ghyll Resr
Skipton
Skipton Moor
Wharfedale
Addingham
Windsover Farm
High Bradley Moor
Middleton
Silsden Moor
A6034
West Park Wood
Denton
Low Bradley
Askwith
River Wharfe
Silsden Resr
Bradley Ings
A629
ILKLEY
Burley in Wharfedale
Silsden
Kildwick

19 TR, no SP (40km/25 miles). Pass SP Unsuitable for Caravans, immediately cross cattle grid and cycle along unfenced road. Cross another cattle grid and continue along this now single track walled road. Cycle through Hawkswick towards Arncliffe.

20 TL at TJ, SP Kilnsey/Grassington. Enter Arncliffe and cross River Skirfare. TR just after the bridge (effectively SO), beside the width limit SP.

21 LHF at village green. Pass telephone box and post office. TR at TJ (effectively SO), SP Kilnsey/Grassington (43.5km/27 miles). Pass Hawkswick Cote Caravan Park on right. Continue.

22 TR at TJ onto B6160, SP Grassington/ Skipton (48.5km/30 miles). Cycle through Kilnsey and continue along B6160, passing Kilnsey Park and Trout Farm. Arrive Threshfield.

23 TL, SP Grassington/Pateley Bridge (55km/34 miles). Then TR staying on B6160, SP Burnsall. Cycle under railway bridge, through Burnsall and Barden, passing Barden Tower on left (65km/40.5 miles). Continue on B6160, past Strid Wood and Bolton Abbey, under the distinctive arch and retrace your route under the old bridge, SP Beamsley Lane, back onto the A59.

24 TR, SP Beamsley (72.5km/45 miles). Pass through Beamsley (no SP) and along a quiet, flat lane, eventually through a golf course.

25 TR at TJ into Longbar Road, no SP.

79km (49 miles)

26 TR at XR into Middleton Avenue, no SP. Recross the A65. TL at TJ and finish the route at the town hall. ***80.5km (50 miles)***

Food and drink

Lots of choice in Ilkley, Grassington and Kettlewell, a convenience store and tearoom in Bolton Abbey village, pubs in Appletreewick, Arncliffe, Kilnsey and Burnsall, and convenience stores in Hebden and Threshfield.

Cavendish Pavilion, Bolton Abbey Estate

A large purpose built café at the entrance to Strid Wood. Also gift shop and displays on the estate and Strid Wood.

Barden Tower Tearoom, Bolton Abbey Estate

Located in a 15th-century priests house, adjacent to Barden Tower.

Places of interest along the route

A Bolton Abbey Estate, near Skipton

Bolton Abbey Estate is the Yorkshire estate of the Duke and Duchess of Devonshire. It comprises moorland and woodland, many miles of footpaths and nature trails. The River Wharfe runs through the estate and is famous for its trout fishing and wildlife. Overlooking the river are the imposing ruins of a 12th-century **priory** and a restored and thriving parish church. Strid Wood sits alongside the river, close to the Strid, a spectacular point where the river surges

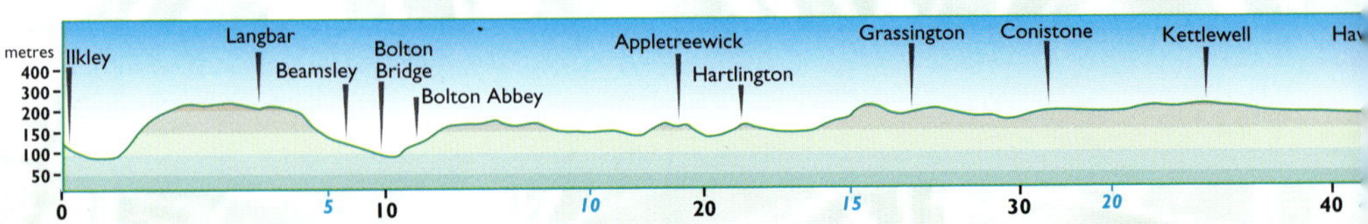

River Wharfe at Ilkley

through a narrow gorge. Further north are the ruins of the impressive 15th-century shooting lodge, **Barden Tower**. The estate is open all year but the opening times of the various tearooms/restaurants should be confirmed by telephone. Admission free. Telephone (01756) 710533.

B Upper Wharfedale Folk Museum, Grassington

Grassington is a picturesque small town. The Folk Museum is located in two 18th-century lead miners' cottages in the town square and depicts the life and history of Upper Wharfedale. There are exhibits on lead mining, minerals, tools, farming, period costumes, folklore, the railway and World War II memorabilia. Open April to September, daily 1400–1630; October to March, Saturday and Sunday 1400–1630. Nominal charge. For further information, telephone Grassington National Park/Tourist Information Centre on (01756) 752774.

C Kilnsey Park and Trout Farm, Kilnsey

Visitors can view and feed the fish. Also conservation centre, nature trail, fly fishing, horse riding, radio controlled boats, herb centre, restaurant and café. Open all year, daily 0900–1730 (or dusk if earlier). Charge for activities. Telephone (01756) 752150.

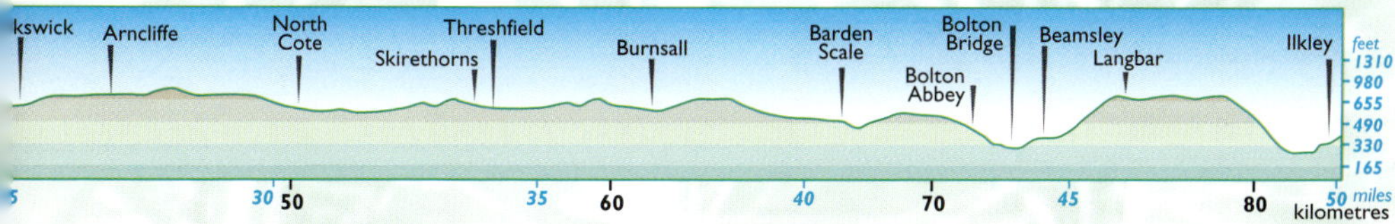

Route 23 THE WESTERN DALES – KIRKBY LONSDALE TO SEDBERGH

Route information

Distance 85km (53 miles)

Grade Strenuous

Terrain Quiet lanes and a few stretches of A road, climbs and descents.

Time to allow 5–9 hours.

Getting there by car Kirkby Lonsdale is on the A65, in the south western Dales. Parking is available in the market place (opposite the Tourist Information Centre), daily except Thursday (market day).

Getting there by train There is no practical railway access to this ride.

From Kirkby Lonsdale a quiet road north follows the River Lune along the western edge of the Dales. The route continues up to Tebay and then heads east to Ravenstonedale. From here you head west then south, mostly on an A road, to reach the pretty town of Sedbergh, and then continue with a lovely ride along Dentdale. The route cuts south just before Dent (although the short diversion to Dent is worth the effort). A hard climb leads to a pleasant descent along Barbondale and back into Kirkby Lonsdale.

Places of interest along the route

A Kirkby Lonsdale

Kirkby Lonsdale is a traditional market town with market square and 600-year-old cross, situated on the banks of the River Lune. The main street and its surrounds are worth exploring. Turner painted the view from the churchyard of the Lune Valley and Ruskin described it as 'one of the loveliest scenes in England'. Nearby Devil's Bridge, on the return route, is thought to be at least 600 years old.

B Kelleth Toy Factory, Kelleth

Husband and wife partnership creating hand made wooden toys. Visitors to the workshop are always welcome. Open most days, including weekends, telephone to confirm on (015396) 23248.

C Sedbergh

Surrounded by fells, Sedbergh is an old market town with cobbled streets. There has been a community here for hundreds of years. St Andrews church, originally Norman, has examples of every period of ecclesiastical architecture since then. Just outside Sedbergh is Brigflatts, the oldest complete Quaker Meeting House still in use, with an original oak interior. Open all year, daily. Services held Sundays, 1030. Telephone (015396) 20125.

D Dent

Dent is a beautiful Dales village, with cobbled main street, and a memorial fountain commemorating Professor Adam Sedgwick (1785–1853) who was Professor of Geology at Cambridge and born in Dent. **Dent Craft Centre** is situated in a converted hay barn, just outside the village. There was a print workshop here at one time and a Victorian printing press, in working order, can be seen. There are resident craftspeople at the centre and visitors can see pottery, candle making, metal work and original oil and watercolour painting. Restaurant and B&B. Telephone to confirm opening times on (015396) 25400.

River Lune, Kirkby Lonsdale

Food and drink

There are numerous opportunities for refreshment in Kirkby Lonsdale, Sedbergh and Dent, and pubs in Tebay and Ravonstonedale.

Barnaby Rudge, Tebay
The first building in town. Pub, also serving teas and coffees.

Kings Head Hotel, Ravonstonedale
Pub and hotel with pleasant separate dining area. Good, cheap meals served until 1800.

The Fat Lamb, Ravonstonedale
Traditional pub with open fires, serving bar and restaurant meals. Also small nature reserve.

Route description

Start by the Tourist Information Centre in Kirkby Lonsdale. Follow road to left to avoid one way street (SP No Entry). Follow road as it bends to right, SP Old Town. TL at TJ, SP Old Town/Old Hutton.

1 TR, SP Rigmaden/Killington. Continue on this flat road, with a good view of the Dales to right.

2 RHF, keeping to the flat road (4.5km/3 miles). Continue north.

3 TR at XR, opposite SP Dead End, and descend hedged road.

4 TL at TJ, SP Sedbergh/Kendal.

5 TR at TJ, SP Sedbergh/Hawes/Tebay (15km/9.5 miles). Cross bridge over River Lune.

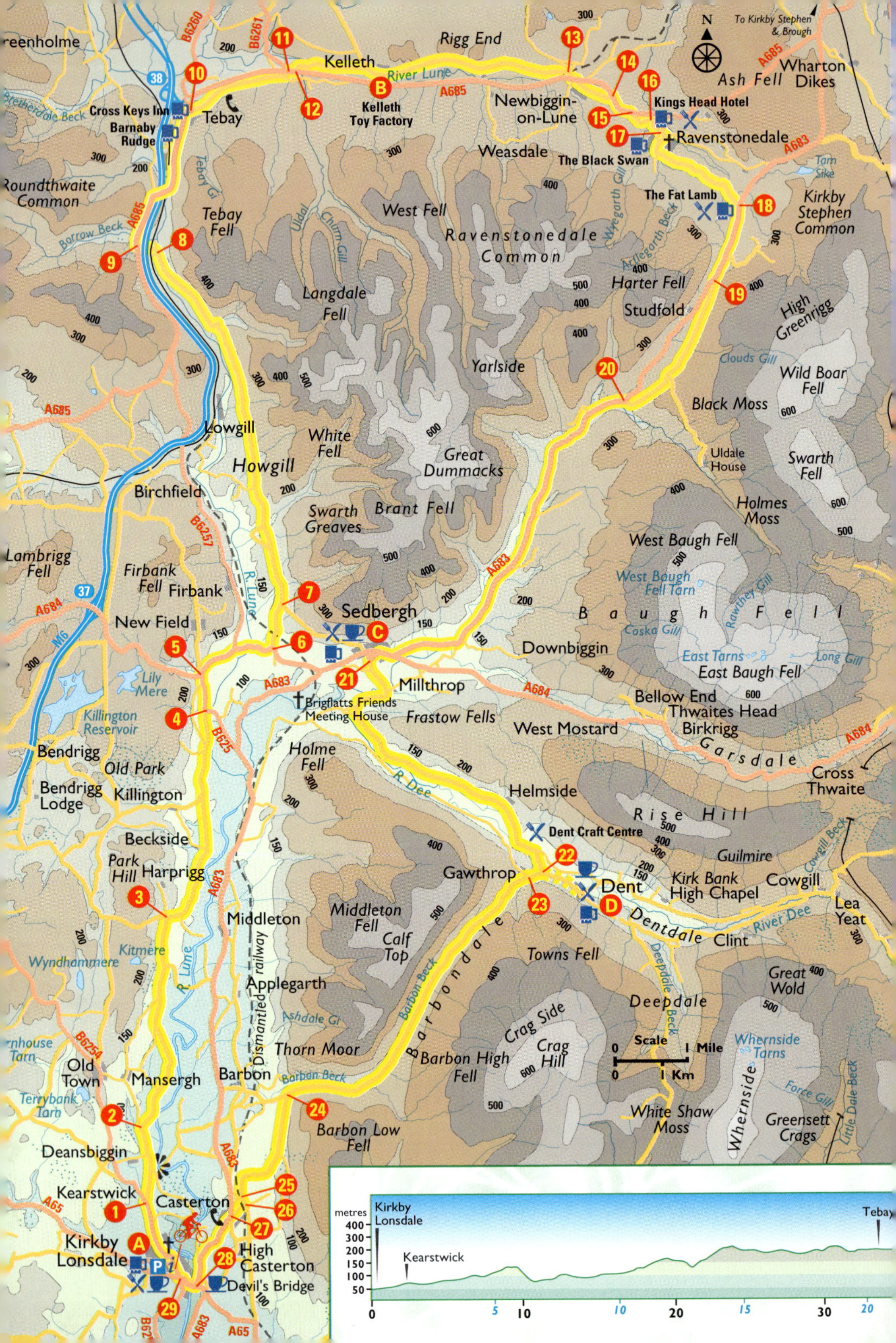

To Kirkby Stephen & Brough
N
Greenholme
B6260
B6261
Rigg End
Kelleth
River Lune
A685
Kelleth Toy Factory
Newbiggin-on-Lune
Ash Fell
Wharton Dikes
Kings Head Hotel
Ravenstonedale
The Black Swan
Weasdale
Cross Keys Inn
Tebay
Barnaby Rudge
Roundthwaite Common
Tebay Gill
Tebay Fell
Borrow Beck
West Fell
Ravenstonedale Common
The Fat Lamb
Tarn Sike
Kirkby Stephen Common
Wyegarth Gill
Artlegarth Beck
Uldale
Churn Gill
Langdale Fell
Harter Fell
Studfold
High Greenrigg
Clouds Gill
Yarlside
Wild Boar Fell
Black Moss
Lowgill
White Fell
Great Dummacks
Uldale House
Swarth Fell
Howgill
Birchfield
Holmes Moss
Swarth Greaves
Brant Fell
West Baugh Fell
B6257
Lambrigg Fell
Firbank Fell
Firbank
R. Lune
West Baugh Fell Tarn
Rawthey Gill
Baugh Fell
A684
M6
New Field
Sedbergh
Coska Gill
Downbiggin
East Tarns
Long Gill
East Baugh Fell
Lily Mere
A683
Millthrop
Bellow End
Thwaites Head
Brigflatts Friends Meeting House
Frastow Fells
Killington Reservoir
West Mostard
Birkrigg
B625
Garsdale
Bendrigg
Old Park
Holme Fell
Cross Thwaite
R. Dee
Bendrigg Lodge
Killington
Helmside
Rise Hill
Beckside
Dent Craft Centre
Guilmire
Park Hill
Harprigg
Gawthrop
Dent
Kirk Bank
High Chapel
Cowgill
Cowgill Beck
Middleton
Middleton Fell
Dentdale
Clint
River Dee
Lea Yeat
Calf Top
Towns Fell
Wyndhammere
Kitmere
R. Lune
Dismantled railway
Barbondale
Deepdale Beck
Great Wold
Applegarth
Barbon Beck
Crag Side
Deepdale
Ashdale Gi
Whernside Tarns
Thorn Moor
Scale
1 Mile
1 Km
B6254
Barbon High Fell
Crag Hill
Old Town
Mansergh
Barbon
Barbon Beck
Force Gill
Whernside
Terrybank Tarn
Barbon Low Fell
White Shaw Moss
Greensett Crags
Little Dale Beck
Deansbiggin
A683
Kearstwick
Casterton
A65
Kirkby Lonsdale
High Casterton
Devil's Bridge
B6254
A683
A65
metres
Kirkby Lonsdale
Kearstwick
Tebay
400
350
300
250
200
150
100
50
0
5
10
10
20
15
30
20

6 TL, no SP except height restriction sign (17km/10.5 miles). Climb and pass under old railway bridge.

7 TL at TJ, SP Howgill. Cross bridge and climb. Continue on this road. Cross cattle grid at 23km (14.5 miles); cross another cattle grid and bridge (25km/15.5 miles). At 27km (17 miles) cross large bridge and shortly after:

8 TR at TJ, no SP (TL is into a farm). Pass under railway bridge and M6.

9 TR at TJ, SP Tebay/Orton. Cross over M6. Continue into Tebay. ***30km (18.5 miles)***

10 TR as road bends to left, no SP. Pass tennis courts on left. Follow road as it swings to left (telephone on right).

11 TR at TJ onto A685, SP Brough/Kirkby Stephen.

12 TL, SP Rousbeck/Kelleth (34.5km/21.5 miles). Continue through Kelleth (passing Toy Factory on right) and on to Newbiggin-on-Lune. ***41km (25.5 miles)***

13 TR at TJ, no SP. Immediately TL at TJ, SP Kirkby Stephen/Brough A685. Then TR almost immediately, SP Newbiggin-on-Lune.

14 TR at TJ, SP Brough A685.

15 TR, SP Ravenstonedale, and enter village.

16 TR, SP Ravenstonedale.

17 TR at TJ, SP Sedbergh/A683 (44km/27.5 miles). Follow road as it bends to right, pass the Methodist and then the United Reformed church on right. As road bends left, follow SP Sedbergh.

18 TR at TJ onto A683, SP Sedbergh.

19 TL, SP Fell End/Uldale (49km/30.5 miles). This is a quieter road with a steep descent to:

20 TL at TJ onto A683, no SP. Continue into Sedbergh. ***61.5km (38 miles)***

21 TR at TJ for the town centre and Brigflatts. Otherwise, TL at TJ, SP Dent/Motorway/Kendal/Kirkby Lonsdale/ Lancaster. Cross bridge and follow SP Dent/Cumbria Cycle Way. Continue on this road. Pass Dent Craft Centre on left.

22 To visit Dent, SO and cycle 1km (0.6 mile) into village. After visit retrace route and TL, SP Gawthrop/Barbon. Otherwise, TR, SP Gawthrop/Barbon (70km/43.5 miles), and climb.

23 TL, SP Barbon/Kirkby Lonsdale. Climb over Barbon Beck, then descend.

24 TL, SP Casterton/Kirkby Lonsdale (78.5km/49 miles). Cross a cattle grid and enter woods.

25 TL at TJ, SP Cowan Bridge/Settle.

26 TR at XR, SP Casterton (82km/51 miles). Pass under old railway bridge.

27 TL at TJ onto A683, no SP. Pass telephone on right, Information Point and Devil's Bridge (can walk across bridge to avoid next junction).

28 TR at TJ, SP Kendal.

29 TR, SP Town Centre, and finish the route at the Tourist Information Centre.

85km (53 miles)

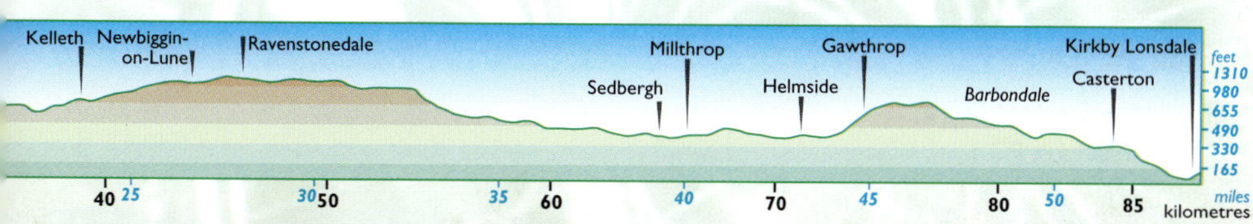

Route 24

BARNARD CASTLE AND SWALEDALE

Route information

Distance 88.5km (55 miles)

Grade Strenuous

Terrain Climbs and descents, valleys and hilltops. Four sections of off-road, varying from a green lane to a rocky track.

Time to allow 6–10 hours.

Getting there by car Barnard Castle is on the north edge of the Yorkshire Dales. Take the A67 from the A66 Appleby to Darlington road. There is a free long term car park near the centre of town.

Getting there by train There is no practical railway access to this ride.

From Barnard Castle the route heads south east through a series of small hamlets and pretty lanes. A climb over a high moor leads into Swaledale – although quieter than the more popular Wensleydale, there is still traffic on this through road and three sections of delightful off-road on downhill tracks give a car free ride. After skirting Keld, the barns of West Stones Dale and the bleakness of Tan Hill provide a suitable contrast to the previous countryside. A final piece of off-road leads to Bowes before a section of A road back to Barnard Castle.

Route description

Start from the Tourist Information Centre in Barnard Castle. Pass the Methodist Church on right and TR at TJ (effectively SO), SP Bowes/Brough. Cycle through the town and SO at roundabout, SP Bowes. At bottom of hill, cross bridge and TL at TJ, SP Reeth/Richmond/Scotch Corner. Continue.

1 SO at staggered XR, SP Brignall (4km/2.5 miles). Cross A66 and cycle along a narrow lane.

2 TR at TJ, SP A66. Cross bridge controlled by traffic lights.

3 TR, SP Barningham (10km/6 miles). Climb.

4 TL at TJ, SP Newsham.

5 Arrive Newsham. TR at XR, SP Dalton/Gayles. ***15.5km (9.5 miles)***

6 Arrive Dalton and TR at TJ, SP Gayles/Kirby Hill/Richmond. Then, TL, SP Richmond. Continue through Gayles (19km/12 miles) and into Kirby Hill. Continue to end of village and sharp bend where:

7 TR at TJ, SP Richmond. ***22km (13.5 miles)***

8 TR, SP Marske/Reeth, and climb, passing firing ranges on right. Reach top of hill (26.5km/16.5 miles) and descend.

9 TR at TJ, no SP. Pass Park Top Farm on left for fast descent. Arrive Marske. Descend and cross bridge.

10 TR at TJ (effectively SO), SP Marrick/Hurst/Reeth (31km/19 miles). Pass seat on right and climb then descend.

Swaledale

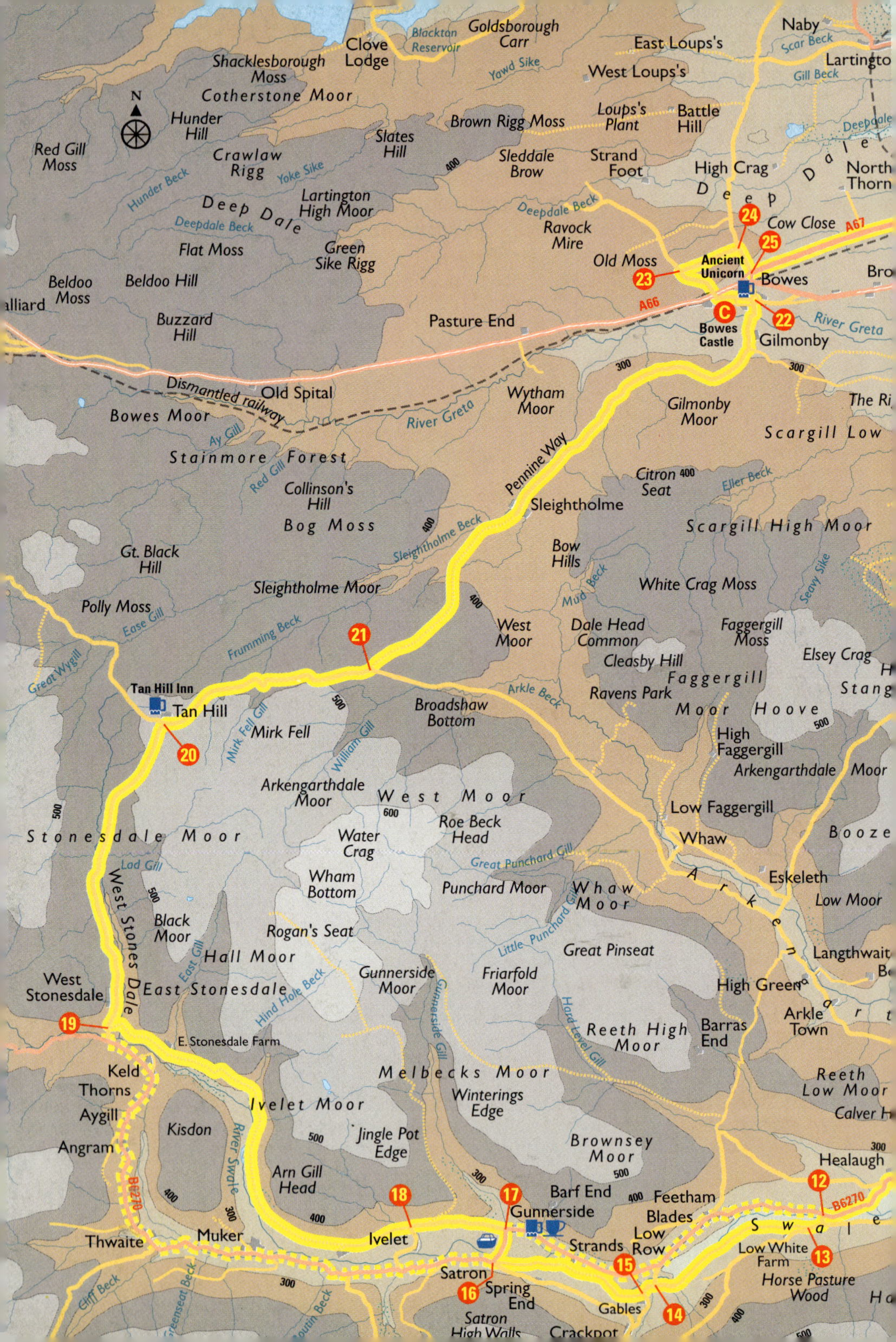

Shacklesborough Moss
Clove Lodge
Blackton Reservoir
Goldsborough Carr
Naby
East Loups's
Scar Beck
Lartington
Cotherstone Moor
Yawd Sike
West Loups's
Gill Beck
Hunder Hill
Red Gill Moss
Slates Hill
Brown Rigg Moss
Loups's Plant
Battle Hill
Deepdale
Crawlaw Rigg
Yoke Sike
Hunder Beck
Sleddale Brow
Strand Foot
High Crag
North Thorn
Deep Dale
Lartington High Moor
Deepdale Beck
Cow Close
A67
Flat Moss
Green Sike Rigg
Ravock Mire
Old Moss
Ancient Unicorn
Bowes
Beldoo Moss
Beldoo Hill
Buzzard Hill
A66
Bowes Castle
Pasture End
River Greta
Gilmonby
Dismantled railway
Old Spital
Wytham Moor
Gilmonby Moor
Bowes Moor
Scargill Low
Ay Gill
Pennine Way
Stainmore Forest
Red Gill
Collinson's Hill
Citron Seat
Eller Beck
Sleightholme
Bog Moss
Sleightholme Beck
Scargill High Moor
Gt. Black Hill
Bow Hills
Seavy Sike
Sleightholme Moor
Mud Beck
White Crag Moss
Polly Moss
Ease Gill
Frumming Beck
West Moor
Dale Head Common
Faggergill Moss
Great Wygill
Cleasby Hill
Elsey Crag
Tan Hill Inn
Tan Hill
Arkle Beck
Ravens Park
Faggergill Moor
Hoove
Broadshaw Bottom
Mirk Fell Gill
Mirk Fell
William Gill
High Faggergill
Arkengarthdale Moor
Arkengarthdale Moor
West Moor
Roe Beck Head
Low Faggergill
Stonesdale Moor
Water Crag
Whaw
Booze
Lad Gill
Great Punchard Gill
Eskeleth
Wham Bottom
Punchard Moor
Whaw Moor
Low Moor
West Stones Dale
Black Moor
Rogan's Seat
Little Punchard Gill
Arkengarthdale
Langthwaite
Great Pinseat
Hall Moor
East Gill
High Green
West Stonesdale
East Stonesdale
Hind Hole Beck
Gunnerside Moor
Friarfold Moor
Hard Level Gill
Arkle Town
Gunnerside Gill
Reeth High Moor
Barras End
E. Stonesdale Farm
Melbecks Moor
Reeth Low Moor
Keld
Thorns
Aygill
Ivelet Moor
Winterings Edge
Calver Hill
Kisdon
Angram
River Swale
Jingle Pot Edge
Brownsey Moor
Healaugh
Arn Gill Head
Barf End
Feetham
B6270
Gunnerside
Blades
Swale
Thwaite
Muker
Ivelet
Low Row
Strands
Low White Farm
Satron
Spring End
Horse Pasture Wood
Gables
Cliff Beck
Greenseat Beck
Oxnop Beck
Satron High Walls
Crackpot

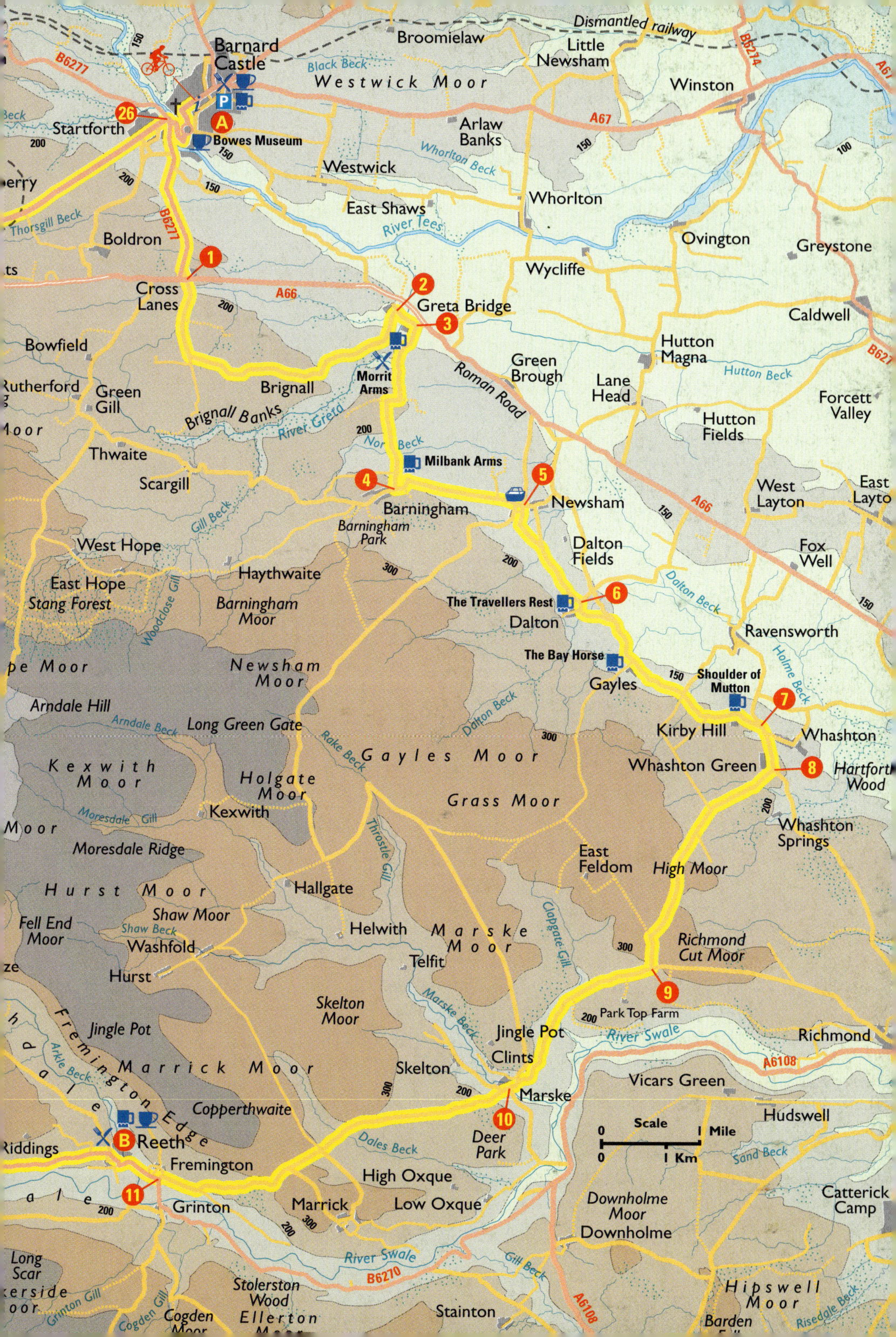
Barnard Castle
Broomielaw
Dismantled railway
Little Newsham
B6274
A67
B6277
Black Beck
Westwick Moor
Winston
Startforth
Bowes Museum
Arlaw Banks
Whorlton Beck
Westwick
East Shaws
Whorlton
River Tees
Thorsgill Beck
Boldron
B6277
Ovington
Greystone
Cross Lanes
A66
Wycliffe
Greta Bridge
Caldwell
Bowfield
Morrit Arms
Brignall
Roman Road
Green Brough
Hutton Magna
Hutton Beck
B6274
Rutherford
Green Gill
Lane Head
Forcett Valley
Brignall Banks
River Greta
Hutton Fields
Thwaite
Nor Beck
Milbank Arms
Scargill
Barningham
Newsham
West Layton
East Layton
Gill Beck
Barningham Park
A66
West Hope
Dalton Fields
Fox Well
East Hope
Stang Forest
Haythwaite
The Travellers Rest
Dalton Beck
Woodclose Gill
Barningham Moor
Dalton
Ravensworth
The Bay Horse
Newsham Moor
Gayles
Shoulder of Mutton
Holme Beck
Arndale Hill
Arndale Beck
Long Green Gate
Dalton Beck
Kirby Hill
Whashton
Kexwith Moor
Rake Beck
Gayles Moor
Whashton Green
Hartforth Wood
Holgate Moor
Kexwith
Grass Moor
Moresdale Gill
Whashton Springs
Moresdale Ridge
Throstle Gill
East Feldom
High Moor
Hurst Moor
Hallgate
Shaw Moor
Fell End Moor
Shaw Beck
Helwith
Marske Moor
Clapgate Gill
Richmond Cut Moor
Washfold
Telfit
Hurst
Fremington Edge
Skelton Moor
Marske Beck
Park Top Farm
River Swale
Richmond
Jingle Pot
Jingle Pot
Clints
A6108
Arkle Beck
Marrick Moor
Skelton
Vicars Green
Marske
Copperthwaite
Hudswell
Reeth
Scale
Mile
Km
Riddings
Deer Park
Dales Beck
Sand Beck
Fremington
High Oxque
Catterick Camp
Grinton
Marrick
Low Oxque
Downholme Moor
Downholme
River Swale
Gill Beck
Long Scar
B6270
Grinton Gill
Stolerston Wood
Hipswell Moor
Cogden Gill
Cogden Moor
Ellerton
Stainton
A6108
Risedale Beck
Barden

11 TR at TJ, SP Reeth (37km/23 miles). Continue through Reeth.

12 To continue route off-road, TL, SP Askrigg (42km/26 miles). Cross bridge to TR at TJ, SP Askrigg. To avoid the off-road sections, continue SO on B6270 through Gunnerside, Muker, Thwaite and on past Keld, where TR just before direction 19, SP West Stonesdale/Tan Hill.

13 Before the road starts to climb, TR at Low White Farm, pass SP Unsuitable for Motors and continue along a well-surfaced green lane, which runs close to the river. Pass through a farm and onto tarmac.

14 To continue route off-road, TL at TJ (effectively SO), SP Crackpot. To rejoin road, TR then TL onto B6270. ***45.5km (28.5 miles)***

15 TR, no SP (beside house called Gables). Pass through lower gate, SP No Cars/ Bridleway Only, and into another green lane, again passing close to the river.

16 TR at TJ, SP Reeth/Richmond. Descend, cross the river and enter Gunnerside.

17 TL just to the right of the Post Office/ Stores (49km/30.5 miles). Climb out of Gunnerside, then descend crossing a small bridge.

18 TR at TJ, no SP but pass a SP No Through Road (51km/31.5 miles). At houses take RHF, passing to right. Continue to end of tarmac and take right hand track to carry on along the level. This firm track leads up the dale to the right of the River Swale. The track crosses a stream and zig-zags upwards (this part may have to be walked) before flattening out again. Pass through a gate next to a waterfall and take RHF, SP Pennine Way. NB: do not take track SP Pennine Way Keld as this is a footpath. Continue up a stony track and through a gate leading to East Stonesdale Farm. Continue on track as it reverts to tarmac and leaves the farm lane.

19 TR at TJ, no SP but pass a yellow grit bin to the right. Continue. ***59km (36.5 miles)***

20 TR at TJ, SP Tan Hill Inn and pass the pub on the left. ***64km (40 miles)***

21 TL, SP Bowes. Pass SP Unsuitable for Motors and cycle along a firm, partially tarmacked track which joins the Pennine Way. Continue on, passing through a gate, past a farm and back onto tarmac. Eventually, arrive Bowes and cross river.

22 TL at XR (roundabout), no SP (78.5km/ 49 miles). Continue along Bowes Main Street, passing Bowes Castle on the left. Follow the Main Street round to the right and over main road.

23 TR at TJ onto a flat road, no SP.

24 TR at TJ, no SP. ***81km (50.5 miles)***

25 TL at TJ onto A67, SP Barnard Castle. Continue into the town.

26 TR at TJ, SP Tourist Information. TL, SP Barnard Castle, cross bridge, pass castle and climb into town. SO at roundabout to return to Tourist Information Centre and complete the route. ***88.5km (55 miles)***

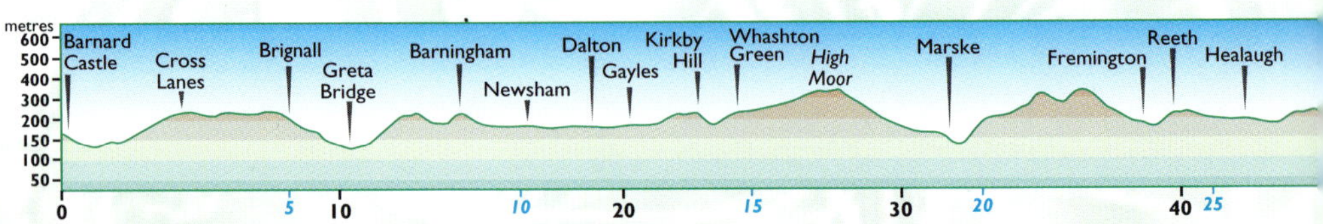

Places of interest along the route

A Barnard Castle

Barnard Castle is an attractive market town. The 12th-century **castle** was built by Bernard Baliol and Bernard's castle gave its name to the town that grew up around it. English Heritage site. Audio tour and gift shop. Picnics welcome. Open April to October, daily 1000–1800 (or dusk if earlier); November to March, Wednesday–Sunday 1000–1300 and 1400–1600. Charge. Telephone 0191-212 3000. The **Bowes Museum** has a varied and magnificent collection of European paintings, furniture, decorative arts, textiles, costume, archaeology and local history. Open all year, Monday–Saturday 1000–1730, Sunday 1400–1700; March, April and October closes 1700; November to February closed 1600. Charge. Café (free admission) open April to October, museum opening times apply. Telephone (01833) 690606. See route 9 for further information.

B Reeth

The village of Reeth is strategically sited at the junctions of Swaledale and Arkengarthdale, the most northerly of the Yorkshire Dales. There is a large village green, which is still the focal point of many traditional events. Market day is on Friday. The **Swaledale Folk Museum** illustrates the local history of the Dales – village life and traditions, religion, farming, mining and knitting, and much more. Gift shop. Open Easter to October, daily 1030–1700. Charge. Telephone (01748) 884373. Crafts have played a large part in the life of the Dales and craftworkers, located in the **Dales Centre**, continue the tradition of producing high quality goods. See route 13 for further information.

Food and drink

Plenty of places in Barnard Castle (and a café at the Bowes Museum) and Reeth. There are pubs in Barningham, Gayles, Kirby Hill and Bowes, and a shop in Newsham. Gunnerside has a shop and tearoom.

Morrit Arms, Greta Bridge
Bar, restaurant and hotel. Bar meals served.

The Travellers Rest, Dalton
A pub with a decidedly French feel. The Tricolor is flown and a Citroen 2CV is parked outside.

Tan Hill Inn, Tan Hill
England's highest pub at 528m (1732 feet). Morning coffee, bar snacks and meals served.

C Bowes Castle, Bowes

Originally the site of a Roman fort on the York to Carlisle Road. The castle came into the Crown's possession in 1171 and was first invaded by the Scots in 1174. It suffered many invasions from Robert the Bruce during the 14th century. English Heritage property. Access at all reasonable times. Admission free. Telephone 0171-973 3000 for further information.

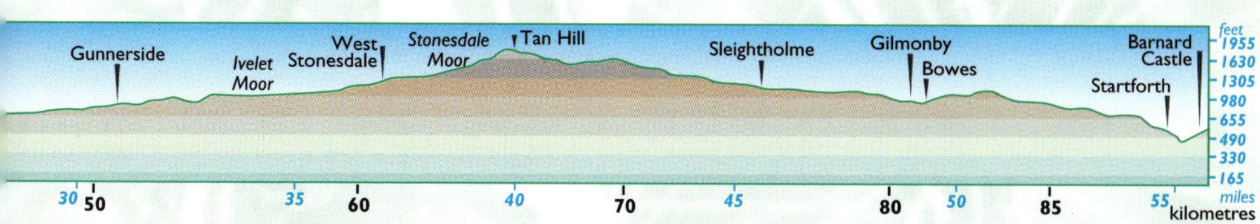

Route 25

WESTERN AND NORTHERN DALES – A GRANDE RANDONNÉE

Route information

Distance 131km (81.5 miles)

Grade Strenuous

Terrain A wide variety of roads and terrain, incorporating two firm off-road sections.

Time to allow 10 hours minimum. This could easily be used as a weekend route as there is a campsite and accommodation in Horton in Ribblesdale. Telephone the Tourist Information Centre at Pen-y-ghent Café on (01729) 860333 for information.

Getting there by car Kirkby Stephen is to the north west of the Dales, on the A685. There is car parking in the town.

Getting there by train Kirkby Stephen is on the Settle to Carlisle line.

South from Kirkby Stephen, on a section of the Cumbrian Cycleway alongside the River Eden. Then west along Garsdale to Sedbergh. The route now swings east again, along pretty Dentdale to Ribblesdale and the most southerly point of the route at Horton in Ribblesdale. A lovely piece of firm off-road track leads over Birkwith Moor into Langstrothdale. You now continue north, over Fleet Moss, where another off-road section on a Roman road leads towards Hawes. The Buttertubs Pass then takes you into Swaledale for the final part of the route along Birk Dale.

Places of interest along the route

A Kirkby Stephen

Kirkby Stephen was first settled by the Vikings. The Church of St Stephen, built in 1220, has a 16th-century tower, elegant nave and old stones. The 8th-century Loki Stone, one of only two in Europe, has a carving of Loki (a Norse god), showing him as a devil-like figure with horns. There has been a market in Kirkby Stephen since 1351 and the Cloisters, between the church and market place, were once the site of the Butter Market. For further information, contact Kirkby Stephen Tourist Information Centre on (017683) 71199.

B Dent

A charming village located in the secluded valley of Dentdale and watched over by Whernside, the highest peak in the Yorkshire Dales National Park at 736m (2414 feet). The main street retains its original cobbles and colour-washed stone cottages. Dent was the birthplace of Adam Sedgwick (1785–1853), who was Professor of Geology at Cambridge and born in Dent. There is a memorial to him in the centre of the village. The village was once famous for its thriving hand knitting industry and now has some interesting workshops and galleries. Tourist information is available from the Stone Close Restaurant in Dent, or from the Tourist Information Centre in Ingleton, telephone (01524) 241049. **Dent Craft Centre** is situated in a converted hay barn, just outside the village. There was a print workshop here at one time and a Victorian printing press, in working order, can be seen. There are resident craftspeople at the centre and visitors can see pottery, candle making, metal work and original oil and watercolour painting. Restaurant and B&B. Telephone to confirm opening times on (015396) 25400.

C Ribblehead Viaduct

Ribblehead Viaduct is one of the Settle–Carlisle line's 20 major viaducts. It is one of the best known and probably the most photographed, with its 24 arches spanning Batty Moss below, the site of a former navvy encampment. For further information, telephone the Settle–Carlisle information line on (0660) 660607 or National Rail Enquiries on (0345) 484950.

D Hawes

Market towns are a particular feature of the Yorkshire Dales and Hawes is said to be the highest market town in England. Tuesday is market day and there are several craft workshops. The **Dales Countryside Museum** explains how the people of the Dales have influenced the evolution of the distinctive Dales landscape. There are exhibits on upland farming, wool and hand-knitting (once a major industry in the area), lead mining, stone cutting, dairying and cheesemaking. Hands-on displays and a Time Tunnel, illustrating 10,000 years of Dales history. Gift shop. Open April to October, daily 1000–1700; limited winter opening – telephone for details. Charge. Telephone (01969) 667450. At the **Hawes Ropemakers**, located next to the Countryside Museum, visitors can see traditional ropemaking and learn how the many thin strands of yarn are rapidly twisted into strong rope. The ropeworks manufacture all manner of items, from skipping ropes and dog leads to church bell ropes. Gift shop. Open all year, Monday–Friday 0900–1730; July to October also open Saturday, 1000–1730. Free admission. Telephone (01969) 667487. The **Wensleydale Creamery** manufactures real Wensleydale cheese – there is a viewing gallery overlooking the manufacturing area, a museum explaining the history of Wensleydale cheese and a food hall. Guided tours, audio-video presentation, restaurant and coffee shop. The best time to see cheesemaking is between 1030 and 1500. Open all year, Monday–Saturday 0930–1700, Sunday 1000–1630. Charge. Telephone (01969) 667664.

E Buttertubs Pass

The Buttertubs Pass lies between Hardraw and Muker and is an exhilarating 526m (1726 feet) above sea level. The Buttertubs themselves are four deep holes in the limestone.

Food and drink

There are plenty of places for refreshment in Kirkby Stephen, Sedbergh, Dent, Horton in Ribblesdale and Hawes, including the Wensleydale Creamery. Nateby, Dentdale and Simonestone have pubs; there are tearooms at Dent Craft Centre and Thwaite; Garsdale has a small shop.

Moorcock Inn, near Garsdale Low Moor
Bar and restaurant meals available.

Scow Cottage
Bed and breakfast serving tea and cakes. Delightful setting, with seating inside or out. Open when signposted.

Caravan, Ribble Head
Caravan serving tea, coffee and snacks, with a marvellous view of the Ribblehead Viaduct.

The Station Inn, Ribble Head
Bed and breakfast, real ale and garden. Meals served daily.

Golden Lion Hotel, Horton in Ribblesdale
Hotel and pub. Real ale, and bar and restaurant meals.

Pen-y-ghent Café, Horton in Ribblesdale
On the Pennine way. Tearoom selling large mugs of tea, hot chocolate and coffee together with food. Also Tourist Information Centre. Closed Tuesday.

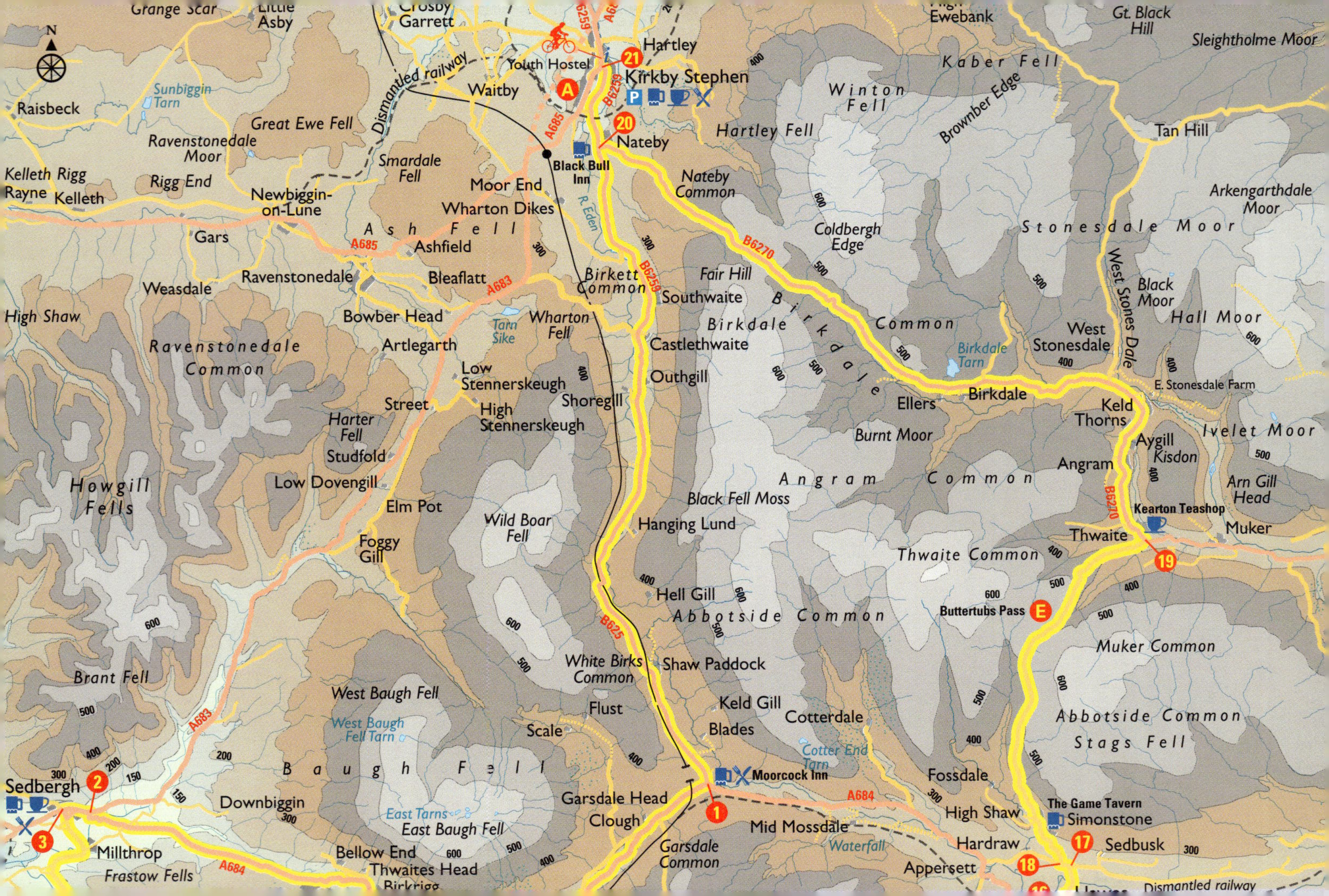
N
Grange Scar
Little Asby
Crosby Garrett
Hartley
Youth Hostel
Kirkby Stephen
Waitby
Dismantled railway
Raisbeck
Sunbiggin Tarn
Great Ewe Fell
Ravenstonedale Moor
Smardale Fell
Nateby
Black Bull Inn
Kelleth Rigg
Rayne
Kelleth
Rigg End
Newbiggin-on-Lune
Moor End
Wharton Dikes
R. Eden
Gars
Ash Fell
Ashfield
A685
B6259
B6270
Weasdale
Ravenstonedale
Bleaflatt
A683
Birkett Common
Southwaite
High Shaw
Bowber Head
Tarn Sike
Wharton Fell
Ravenstonedale Common
Artlegarth
Castlethwaite
Outhgill
Low Stennerskeugh
Street
High Stennerskeugh
Shoregill
Harter Fell
Studfold
Low Dovengill
Howgill Fells
Elm Pot
Wild Boar Fell
Foggy Gill
Hanging Lund
Black Fell Moss
Hell Gill
Abbotside Common
B6259
Brant Fell
White Birks Common
Shaw Paddock
West Baugh Fell
Flust
Keld Gill
Cotterdale
Blades
West Baugh Fell Tarn
Scale
Baugh Fell
Cotter End Tarn
Moorcock Inn
Sedbergh
Downbiggin
Garsdale Head
A684
Clough
East Tarns
East Baugh Fell
Mid Mossdale
Milthrop
Bellow End
Thwaites Head
Birkrigg
Garsdale Common
Waterfall
Frostow Fells
Ewebank
Kaber Fell
Winton Fell
Browber Edge
Hartley Fell
Tan Hill
Gt. Black Hill
Sleightholme Moor
Nateby Common
Arkengarthdale Moor
Coldbergh Edge
Stonesdale Moor
Black Moor
Hall Moor
Fair Hill
West Stones Dale
Birkdale
Common
West Stonesdale
Birkdale Tarn
E. Stonesdale Farm
Ellers
Birkdale
Keld
Thorns
Burnt Moor
Aygill
Kisdon
Ivelet Moor
Angram Common
Angram
Arn Gill Head
Kearton Teashop
Thwaite
Muker
Thwaite Common
Buttertubs Pass
Muker Common
Abbotside Common
Stags Fell
Fossdale
High Shaw
The Game Tavern
Simonstone
Hardraw
Sedbusk
Appersett
Dismantled railway
A
E
1
2
3
17
18
19
20
21

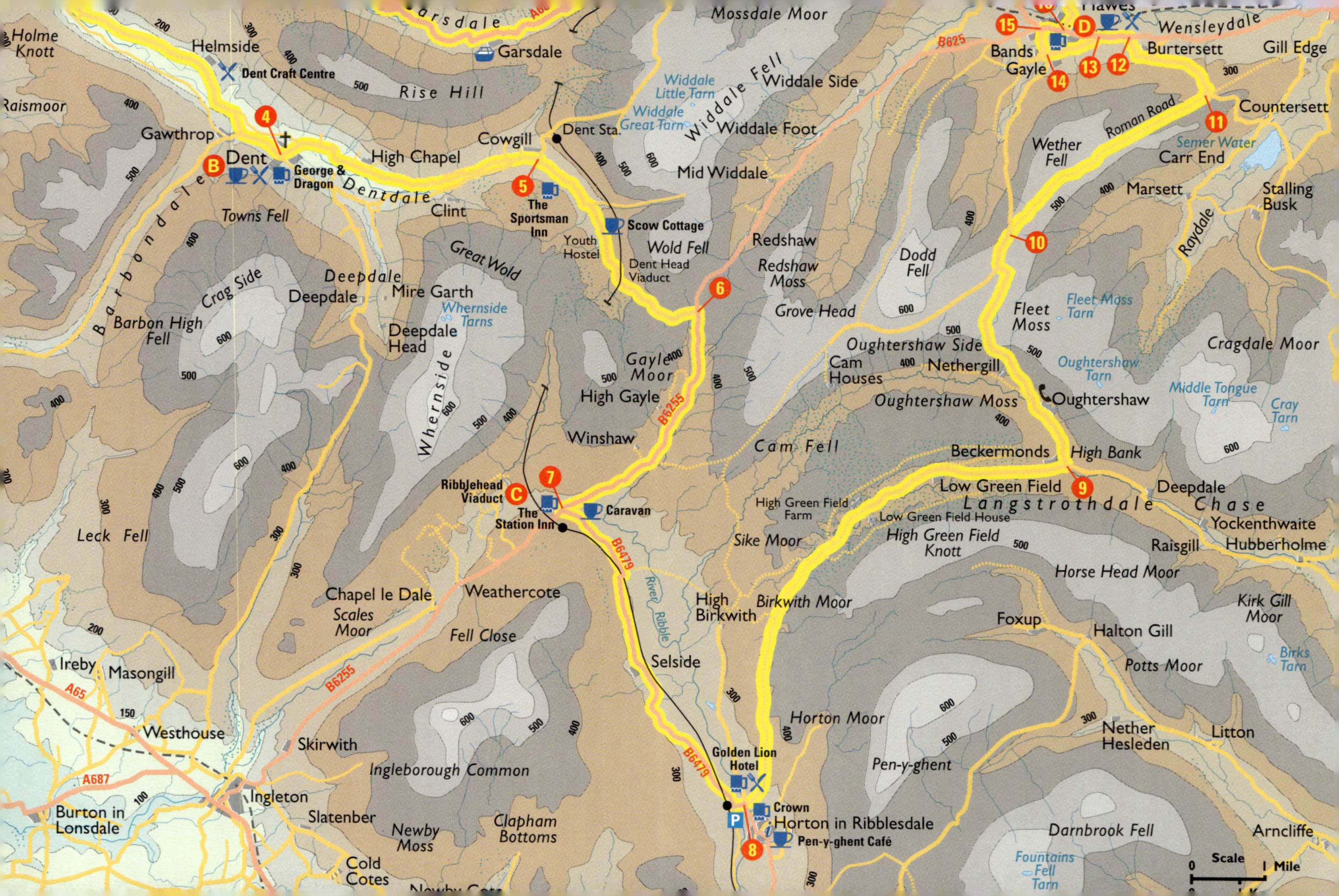
Holme Knott
Helmside
Dent Craft Centre
Garsdale
Rise Hill
Mossdale Moor
Wensleydale
Burtersett
Gill Edge
Bands
Gayle
Raismoor
Gawthrop
Dent
George & Dragon
Dentdale
High Chapel
Cowgill
Dent Sta.
Widdale Little Tarn
Widdale Great Tarn
Widdale Fell
Widdale Side
Widdale Foot
Mid Widdale
Countersett
Wether Fell
Roman Road
Semer Water
Carr End
Marsett
Stalling Busk
Raydale
Barbondale
Towns Fell
Clint
The Sportsman Inn
Scow Cottage
Youth Hostel
Wold Fell
Dent Head Viaduct
Redshaw
Redshaw Moss
Dodd Fell
Great Wold
Crag Side
Deepdale
Mire Garth
Whernside Tarns
Barbon High Fell
Deepdale Head
Whernside
Grove Head
Fleet Moss
Fleet Moss Tarn
Cragdale Moor
Gayle Moor
High Gayle
Oughtershaw Side
Cam Houses
Nethergill
Oughtershaw Tarn
Oughtershaw Moss
Oughtershaw
Middle Tongue Tarn
Cray Tarn
Winshaw
Cam Fell
Beckermonds
High Bank
Ribblehead Viaduct
The Station Inn
Caravan
Low Green Field
Deepdale
Langstrothdale Chase
High Green Field Farm
Low Green Field House
High Green Field Knott
Yockenthwaite
Leck Fell
Sike Moor
Raisgill
Hubberholme
Horse Head Moor
Weathercote
River Ribble
High Birkwith
Birkwith Moor
Chapel le Dale
Scales Moor
Fell Close
Foxup
Halton Gill
Kirk Gill Moor
Selside
Potts Moor
Birks Tarn
Ireby
Masongill
Westhouse
Skirwith
Horton Moor
Nether Hesleden
Litton
Ingleborough Common
Pen-y-ghent
Golden Lion Hotel
Crown
Horton in Ribblesdale
Pen-y-ghent Café
Ingleton
Slatenber
Burton in Lonsdale
Newby Moss
Clapham Bottoms
Darnbrook Fell
Arncliffe
Cold Cotes
Fountains Fell Tarn
A65
A687
B6255
B6479
B625
Scale
0
1 Mile

Route description

Start at Kirkby Stephen Tourist Information Centre. Head along the Main Street, towards the youth hostel situated in the converted church. Pass the youth hostel on the right and TL on the B6259, SP Nateby/Hawes. Climb to Nateby and continue through the village. Cycle along the B6259 (part of the Cumbrian Cycleway), through the valley, following the railway and the River Eden. Pass through Outhgill and continue.

1 TR at TJ onto A684, SP Sedbergh (18.5km/11.5 miles). Under railway bridge and continue along this windy road, with Baugh Fell sloping down to the road on the right. Continue through Garsdale. Cross a cattlegrid (30.5km/19 miles) to enter a section of open moorland, and continue towards Sedbergh.

2 TL at TJ, SP Kendal/Motorway/ Kirkby Lonsdale/Sedbergh.

35km (21.5 miles)

3 TR to go into Sedbergh. Or, TL at TJ, SP Dent/Motorway/Kendal/Kirkby Lonsdale/ Lancaster. Cross bridge and follow SP Dent/ Cumbria Cycle Way. Pass Dent Craft Centre on the left and arrive Dent.

4 TL by the George and Dragon pub (44km/27.5 miles), SP Hawes/Ingleton (via Newby Head). Pass the church on the left and cross bridge. Continue through Cowgill.

49km (30.5 miles)

5 Follow road to right, SP Ingleton/Dent YH. Cross bridge and pass the youth hostel on the right. Dent Head Viaduct is on the left as you climb. Look back for a view. Continue.

6 TR at TJ onto B6255, SP Ingleton/Settle.

56km (35 miles)

7 TL onto B6479, SP Horton in Ribblesdale/ Settle (62.5km/39 miles). Cycle along Ribblesdale, following the line of the railway. Pass through Selside and enter Horton in Ribblesdale (which would make a good overnight stop if cycling this route over two days). Pass the station and round the right hand bend. Cross the bridge over the Ribble, to immediately:

8 TL in front of the Crown pub, no SP (70km/43.5 miles). Cycle through the short car park and climb the walled track (tarmac for the first 20m). Pass the last of the barns on the left and continue through a gateway. The cycling is now mostly flat. Follow the wall on the left, pass through a gateway with iron tied to it and the track opens up. Keep on this well defined track through a gate on the edge of woodland. Cross a cattlegrid and enter the woods (the track is in a wide clearing). Follow this, ignoring track that swings left just before a brief incline. At High Green Field Farm pass through the two gates and continue on to pass Low Green Field House on the right. The track is now tarmac, as you descend along Langstrothdale.

9 TL at TJ opposite a postbox, SP Hawes (83km/51.5 miles). Climb steeply. Pass telephone in small settlement and climb again. Just before the road descends steeply:

10 TR onto an old Roman road, SP Byway Bainbridge (89km/55.5 miles). Initially climb this well-surfaced track, then descend.

11 TL at XR,where track meets tarmac (94.5km/58.5 miles). Descend, soon crossing a bridge on a right hand bend. Pass through Burtersett and descend further.

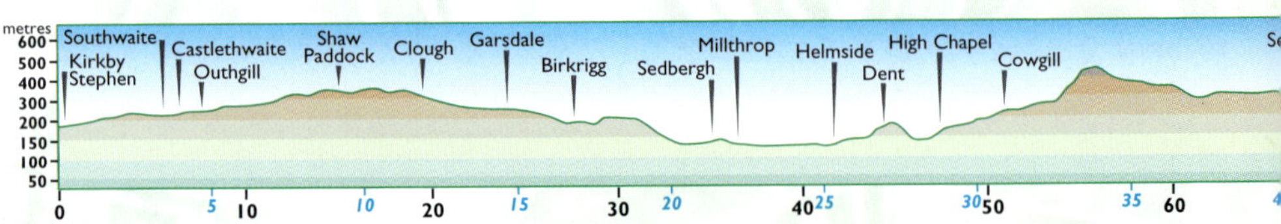

Birkdale

12 TL at TJ, SP Hawes.

13 TL, SP Gayle, and continue into Gayle.

14 TR at TJ, SP Hawes (99km/61.5 miles). Cross bridge and enter Hawes.

15 TR at TJ, SP Aysgarth/Leyburn. Follow road through Hawes, along one way system.

16 TL, SP Hardraw/Muker, and cross river.

17 TL at TJ, SP Hardraw/Muker/ Simonstone/Sedbergh.

18 TR, SP Muker via Buttertubs/ Simonstone. Pass SP 1:6 gradient and climb, crossing cattle grids. Continue to Muker – a lovely view along Swaledale develops as you descend.

19 TL at TJ onto B6270, SP Keld/Kirkby Stephen. Continue on this road, through Thwaite and along Birkdale towards Kirkby Stephen.

20 TR at TJ opposite Black Bull Inn, SP Kirkby Stephen. ***128.5km (80 miles)***

21 TR at TJ, SP Appelby/Brough. Cycle back into Kirkby Stephen, to the Tourist Information Centre and the end of the route. ***131km (81.5 miles)***

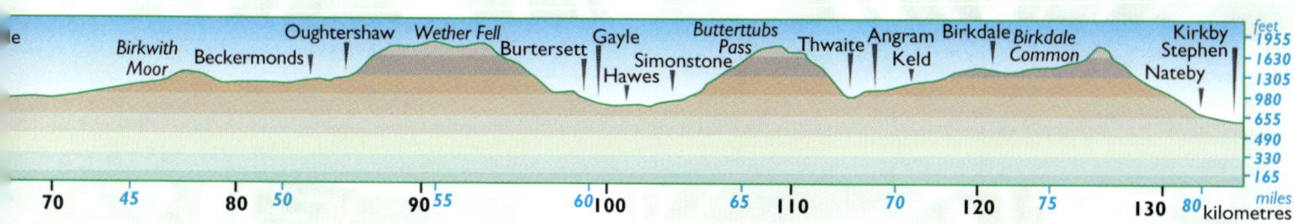

THE CTC

The CTC is Britain's largest national cycling organisation. Founded in 1878, the CTC has over 65,000 members and affiliates throughout the UK, and around 230 local groups. The CTC provides essential services for all leisure cyclists, whether riding on- or off-road, and works to promote cycling and protect cyclists' interests.

Free technical and touring advice

CTC membership makes day-to-day cycling easier. A resident expert cycling engineer answers technical queries about cycle buying, maintenance and equipment. And if you get ambitious about your cycling, the CTC's Touring Department has reams of information about cycling anywhere from Avon to Zimbabwe. Then, when it comes to getting kitted out, the CTC's mail order shop sells a wide variety of clothing and accessories in addition to books, maps and guidebooks, including other titles from HarperCollins.

CTC Helpdesk – telephone (01483) 417217

CTC members also receive *Cycle Touring and Campaigning* magazine free six times a year. *CT&C* takes pride in its journalistic independence. With reports on cycle trips all over the globe, forensic tests on bikes and equipment, and the most vigorous and effective pro-bike campaigning stance anywhere, *CT&C* is required reading for any cyclist.

CTC membership costs from £15 p.a.

It is not just members who benefit. The CTC works on behalf of all Britain's 22 million cycle owners. Its effective campaigning at national level helped to create the Government's National Cycling Strategy. It is lobbying for lower speed limits on country lanes; campaigning so that you can carry bikes on trains; working with Local Authorities to make towns more cycle-friendly, to ensure that roads are designed to meet cyclists' needs and kept well maintained; making sure that bridleways are kept open; and negotiating cyclists' access to canal towpaths.

Whatever kind of cyclist you are – mountain biker, Sunday potterer, bicycle commuter, or out for the day with your family – cycling is easier and safer with the CTC's knowledge and services in your saddlebag. The CTC is the essential accessory for every cyclist!

For further information contact:
CTC
69 Meadrow
Godalming
Surrey
GU7 3HS

Telephone (01483) 417217
Fax (01483) 426994
e-mail: cycling@ctc.org.uk
Website: http://www.ctc.org.uk